# On a Quest for Christ

## Also by Lisa Aré Wulf

Enfolded in God's Arms:
40 Reflections to Embrace Your Inner Healing

# On a Quest for Christ

## Tracing the Footsteps of Your Spiritual Journey

### Second Edition

Lisa Aré Wulf

Spiritual Formation House™
Colorado Springs, Colorado
www.spiritualformationhouse.com

Cover Design by Fresh Vision Design
Interior Design by Wood Nymph Creations
Cover Photograph by Oasis 15 (Shutterstock)
Author Photograph by Duval Digital

Publisher's Cataloging-in-Publication data

Names: Wulf, Lisa Aré, author.
Title: On a quest for Christ : tracing the footsteps of your spiritual journey , second edition / Lisa Aré Wulf.
Description: Colorado Springs, CO: Spiritual Formation House, 2018.
Identifiers: ISBN 978-1-938042-06-5 (Hardcover) | 978-1-938042-04-1 (pbk.) | 978-1-938042-05-8 (Kindle) | 978-1-938042-08-9 (eBook) | LCCN 2018902310
Subjects: LCSH Self-realization--Religious aspects--Christianity. | Prayers and devotions. | Devotional calendars. | Spiritual exercises. | Spirituality. | BISAC RELIGION / Christian Life / Personal Growth
Classification: LCC BV4598.2 .W85 2018 | DDC 248.8/43 -- dc22

Published by Spiritual Formation House™
410A Valley Hi Circle
Colorado Springs, CO 80910
www.spiritualformationhouse.com

Printed in the United States of America

To Calvin

# Contents

# Acknowledgments

*On a Quest for Christ* would not have become a reality without the tireless and exceptional assistance of a truly outstanding group of people.

I am forever indebted to my editor, Kim McCauley, whose suggestions and guidance gave final shape to both editions of this book.

I also appreciate the wise counsel and assistance of many special helpers including Jan Malvern, Susan Defosset, Jerusha Goebel, Judy Downing, Howard Baker, James Ferrier, Anna-Liisa Mullis, Rex Schultz, Jane Fosha, Jennifer Brukiewa, Dave Ruckman, Alice Culp, the Rev. Dr. Barbara Dumke, and Sr. Eileen Currie.

Finally, I am eternally grateful to my loving husband, Calvin Wulf, for his patient encouragement and reassuring presence every step of the way. Thank you, Calvin!

# How to Use this Book

Tracing the footsteps of your spiritual journey can be one of the most illuminating experiences you'll ever have. Consider these aspects as you explore this quest—the quest for Christ.

First, reflect on your goals for the journey:

- Are you searching for your unique sacred path?
- Are you a relatively new believer, seeking a solid spiritual footing?
- Are you seasoned follower of Christ, pursuing a deeper faith?

Next, think about how you would like to take this journey. Consider these options:

- Individual Reflection
- Retreat Experience
- Group Study
- Spiritual Friendship

## Individual Reflection

This devotional guide provides an excellent opportunity to ponder your individual spiritual history. Try these suggestions:

Read the whole book, or choose those chapters that speak to you at this stage of your journey. If you are fairly new to Christianity, the earlier ones may be more relevant. If you've already walked with Jesus for some time, the later chapters can offer extra support.

As you begin each chapter, spend a few moments in silence to calm your mind. Then read through the first several paragraphs. When you reach the section about your story, take time to ponder each question. It may help to write down your thoughts.

Continue reading through the chapter, reflecting on the scripture verses and concluding questions. After the written prayer, silence your mind again and listen for God's response.

Feel free to offer your own personal prayer. Allow it to reflect the thoughts and emotions you experienced in this chapter. Offer your insights and struggles to God.

Give special attention to the Christ Quest Time Map in chapter 29. Consider each step of your journey as you draw the map. Be sure to devote plenty of time to the final chapter as you reflect on your life and the next steps God may have for you.

## Retreat Experience

What is a retreat? It's simply a designated time spent away from your everyday busyness and noise. A retreat doesn't have to be anything fancy, but thoughtful planning helps to assure a fruitful experience. Here are some ideas:

For a short retreat, consider a morning or afternoon get-away. If your schedule allows you to spend a little longer, try two or three days. Whatever the length, make sure you feel comfortable, especially if this is your first personal retreat.

Choose a location free of distractions, preferably away from your regular surroundings. It could be a retreat center, a cabin in the woods, or a nearby park for the afternoon. Any place removed from your day-to-day life is fine.

Make time for silence. Turn off your electronic devices and take a moment to review the previous section on Individual Reflection.

Select chapters that appeal to you and speak to your life experience. Depending on the length of your retreat, you may not be able to complete the entire book. Consider finishing it after you return home.

As you near the end of your retreat, skip forward to chapters 29 and 30. Even if you have not finished all the devotionals, the timeline and reflection questions could be a helpful conclusion to your time away.

## Group Study

*On a Quest for Christ* can easily be adapted for your next group study at church or in another ministry setting. Here are a few questions and suggestions to consider:

Do you want to study the whole book, or concentrate only on specific themes? Either the leader or the group can make this decision and select the most meaningful chapters to accomplish your goals.

How long will your study time be? Do you expect to cover one chapter per session, or several? Will you meet weekly, or on a different schedule?

How will you structure each session? Will the leader facilitate the study, or will it be a joint effort among the group? Is social time included in your meetings? No matter how interesting the discussion is, don't forget to include a period of silence to ponder the reflection questions.

Group members should share only as they feel comfortable without any pressure. Confidentiality is also a must so that all will feel safe. At the initial meeting, establish this ground rule—what is said here stays here. Be sure to remind the group again at later meetings.

At the last session, allow time for the Christ Quest Time Map. And don't skip the last chapter. It will help the participants see where they've been and look forward to the road ahead.

Need help formatting a group study? Consider the Four Session Lesson Plan included at the end of this book.

## Spiritual Friendship

Walking through *On a Quest for Christ* with a spiritual friend or mentor is an excellent way to share both the book and your lives. Here are some possibilities:

You could simply go through the book together, or one of you may guide the discussion. Whichever model you choose, remember that you are equals on this journey.

Both friends can prepare the same chapter and share their insights, or each person can prepare a different chapter and bring it to the discussion. You and your friend may work through the book in sequence, or choose chapters by topic or issue. One person could lead the conversation on a chapter, then the other can serve as leader for the next chapter.

To encourage good listening skills, here is a novel approach you might try:

- Allow the first person to speak uninterrupted for several minutes, sharing thoughts or feelings on the chapter.
- Observe two or three minutes of silence.
- The second person responds with a reflection about the first person's experience.
- Again, keep a few minutes of silence.
- The first person responds to the second person's reflection.
- Finally, reverse the process, allowing second person to share his or her own personal thoughts about the same chapter.

# Opening Thoughts

*May all who search for you*
*be filled with joy and gladness in you.*
*May those who love your salvation*
*repeatedly shout, "The LORD is great!"*
Psalm 40:16 (NLT)

Every day of your life, whether you know it or not, you are on an epic journey. Perhaps you sense a nagging hole in your heart that excitement, money, or love can't fill. Or you may be quite content with your life today, but have a feeling that something else, something deeper, awaits you. Either way, you're on a quest—a quest for Christ.

What is a quest anyway? It is simply a journey toward a worthy goal, the seeking of a noble end. Your way might be full of unexpected twists and heartbreaking turns. Overwhelming challenges may yield a sense of deep joy and peace. In the end, your destination is clear. God's arms are waiting.

This devotional guide is for all who are on a spiritual journey with Christ. Through its pages, you will trace your own steps from the first whispers of faith to a place of rest in God's arms. You may be miles along the road, or you may be just beginning. Regardless of where you are on the journey, your story is sacred—a saga that leads ultimately to God.

During this process, I'll invite you into my personal faith journey. Each chapter features part of my story. Because I've selected just a few snapshots from a lifetime of experience, many people, places, and events are not included. My hope is that the ones I have chosen will lead you to a deeper reflection on your own memories. I've also provided thought-provoking questions, scripture meditations, and special prayers to help you see ever more clearly the transforming grace of God in your life.

As we explore your quest together, reflect on the stages you've passed through. Chances are they won't exactly parallel my own, but the similarities could be surprising. You may have experienced many of the phases, but not all. Perhaps they occurred in a different order. Maybe your unique experiences aren't included in this book. Don't worry; this devotional is only a guide for your journey. As you work through it, you'll see God's hand in your life and the direction he is leading you.

If you want to study this devotional with a group, a spiritual friend, or on a retreat, be sure to check out my suggestions for some creative ideas. I've included them in "How to Use this Book" and the "Four Session Lesson Plan."

As you begin to explore your personal quest for Christ, take a minute to reflect on this scripture passage. Listen for God's message to you.

> *"The Kingdom of Heaven is like a merchant*
> *on the lookout for choice pearls.*
> *When he discovered a pearl of great value,*
> *he sold everything he owned and bought it!"*
> *Matthew 13:45-46 (NLT)*

When we find the treasure we have been seeking for so long, it changes our lives. We hold it close, vowing to never let it go. As we begin to map your quest for the pearl of great value, let's join in prayer, asking for guidance on the journey.

> Jesus—you are the missing piece in our lives, the priceless pearl we seek. For years, we have looked high and low for you. We've searched in every imaginable place. But you've been with us all along, nudging us forward, shepherding us into your flock. Stay with us as we tell our stories and map our spiritual quests. Keep us safe as we continue to seek you on the journey of life, today and always. Amen.

I wish you a fruitful walk filled with joy and wonder, discovery and delight.

CHAPTER 1

# *Birthing*

*The LORD called me before my birth;*
*from within the womb he called me by name.*
*Isaiah 49:1b (NLT)*

"Hey — it's freezing cold out here. And what's with the bright lights and noise? Everything was peaceful and calm until a minute ago!"

No doubt about it, birth is a shock to our little bodies! We suddenly appear on the scene, often to great fanfare and festivity. Then real life sets in. Who will nurture and guide us? What will the future be like? Who will this tiny soul grow up to be?

Your spiritual journey began on the day of your birth. Some of us are born into warm, loving homes. Some are not. Some families are followers of Christ. Some are not. They may be rich or poor, large or small, spiritually strong or emotionally damaged. Regardless of the situation, God tenderly holds each new life in his hand.

## My Story

The stained-glass window sparkled behind my long, white baby dress. Back then, baptism seemed like the socially correct thing to do. So, even though they weren't particularly interested in Christianity, my parents arranged a ceremony at the National Cathedral in Washington, D.C.

Dad was drafted not long after I was born, and the Army assigned him to Walter Reed Hospital in Maryland. Later, after finishing his studies at the Mayo Clinic, he became a brain surgeon in Wyoming. But his professional success did not bring happiness. Alcohol, drugs, violence, and mental illness ravaged our family and wounded my young soul.

Eventually my parents divorced, and our well-to-do lifestyle vanished. Mother moved the four kids to Colorado and re-married. Life seemed disconnected and relationships were strained. Necessities like toilet paper were sometimes hard to come by. Rats lived in the kitchen. Each day brought a new challenge.

## Encouragement

From the moment of birth, God has a faith journey in mind for each of us. Sometimes he gives us a head start by placing us in a Christian family. But even when we grow up clearly outside the realm of faith, he offers a path to make the journey back to him.

Each of us begins the trek as a blank slate, waiting for the hand of God to write a beautiful story with our life. He calls us by name from the beginning, no matter how far we must walk to meet him again. He honors the journey in every life.

## Your Story

How would you describe the household in which you grew up?

What were some good aspects of your childhood?

Describe a few challenges you and your family faced.

Did you have any early childhood religious experience? What was it?

## Reflection

God himself created each of us at this particular time in history for a unique reason. Your birth was not just a random occurrence. Consider your life as you ponder this verse:

> *Even before he made the world,*
> *God loved us and chose us in Christ*
> *to be holy and without fault in his eyes.*
> *Ephesians 1:4 (NLT)*

Can you tell that you are chosen by God? How?

What other thoughts do you have about your birth?

## A Special Prayer

Jesus—before I drew my first breath and opened my eyes to the light, you were there. And you've been with me ever since, through triumphant victories and heartbreaking losses. Let's explore my spiritual story together. I want to see how your steady hand has guided my path. Amen.

# CHAPTER 2

# *Ignoring*

*God looks down from heaven on all mankind*
*to see if there are any who understand,*
*any who seek God.*

*Psalm 53:2 (NIV)*

How far must we run to get away from God? To the end of
the block? Across the state? Around the world? You know the
truth: no matter how far we travel, he's always there. We just
don't recognize him. We're often too busy doing our own
thing, choosing our own destiny. Freedom is our buzzword
and our hoped-for reality.

How do we ignore a God who is everywhere? That seems
easy enough. Being "rational people," we make our own
decisions about what's right for us. That way, we're free to
create our own God or worship none at all.

❧   ❧   ❧   ❧   ❧   ❧   ❧

## My Story

One day, Mother announced, "We're starting a church in our basement. It's going to be a place where people can believe whatever they want." My ten-year-old mind understood that God would be optional. I could take him or leave him. I decided to leave him.

Our little congregation grew and eventually bought a building. During Sunday school, we visited other churches and joked about them later. Why did the Catholic priest wear such strange clothes? And how come the Pillar of Fire Holy Roller Church was just a vacant lot? Maybe it burned down.

All that mattered at our do-it-yourself church was to be a good moral person. It felt more like a discussion group than a church. We had some interesting rituals. The most colorful one occurred on Easter Sunday, when everyone, including the men, dressed up in women's hats, gloves, and purses and paraded around the pews. Communion was a basket of raisins. Someone wrote God out of the hymnal.

## Encouragement

Let's ask again. Can we ignore God? No, not really. We can run, and we can hide, but we can never escape his reality. So, why even try? The farther we travel from him, the longer and more difficult the road back home will be.

But just because we ignore him doesn't mean God isn't with us. He has known about our doubts and wanderings from the beginning. God is patient. He will wait as long as it takes for us to turn and run back to his loving arms.

## Your Story

Have you ever doubted God or walked away from him? When?

If you've questioned the Christian faith, what were your doubts?

Did you choose to believe something else instead? What was it?

How do you imagine God felt about the direction you chose?

## Reflection

When we stray from God's path and make up our own beliefs, it's like building a house on sand that won't stand up to the storms of life. Pray for a moment about this passage:

> *Such is the destiny of all who forget God;*
> *so perishes the hope of the godless.*
> *What they trust in is fragile;*
> *what they rely on is a spider's web.*
> *They lean on the web, but it gives way;*
> *they cling to it, but it does not hold.*
> *Job 8:13-15 (NIV)*

How are you building a life that is stronger than a spider web?

What other thoughts do you have about ignoring God?

## A Special Prayer

Jesus—why did I think I could ignore you? Even when I've walked away, you've waited patiently for me to return. It's time for me to turn around and meet your gaze, face to face. Please hold my hand as I gingerly take my first steps back to you. I want to walk with you forever. Amen.

# CHAPTER 3

# *Awakening*

*Wake up, my heart!*
*Wake up, O lyre and harp!*
*I will wake the dawn with my song.*
Psalm 57:8 (NLT)

Wake up! Get going. It's a crisp new morning without a care on the horizon. All is wonderful as we munch our breakfast cereal, chatting with Jesus Christ, our newfound friend. Hmmm…what's wrong with this picture? Is this really how the spiritual journey works?

Few of us get up one day and instantly become joyful, enthusiastic believers. It usually takes years of searching, trial and error, and launching little test balloons. Faith is a long walk in the same direction that begins with a first step, however halting it may be.

ა ა ა ა ა ა ა

## My Story

Although I wasn't raised as a Christian, I had heard about Jesus. One day when I was about ten, I decided to color a "paint-by-number" picture of him. When it was finished, I challenged him to come down from heaven, pick it up, and take it back with him. Each morning when I woke up, it was still there. After a while, I gave up and put it away.

A few years later, while reading the book, Little Women, I was fascinated by a character who created her own private devotional area in a closet. I was strangely attracted to a secret prayer room complete with a Bible and cross. Somehow, though, I never got around to setting one up for myself.

As a teenager, I saw a film that lingered in my thoughts for years. *Becket* was the true story of a man murdered for his faith in the year 1170. It touched something deep in my soul. I begged to go back to the theater the next night, but Mother said no. I never forgot it. Years later, it was the first video I ever bought.

ა ა ა ა ა ა ა

## Encouragement

The Holy Spirit plants a seed of faith in every soul. For some there is just the right combination of water, soil, and light. The seed sprouts right away, and a tender young plant is encouraged to grow in the life of a seeker.

But often the seed lies dormant, waiting for an opportunity to develop. It may take years or even decades. But God isn't worried. He tenderly holds the precious soul in his hands, waiting for a glimmer of understanding, a flicker of faith.

## Your Story

Do you have a spiritual awakening story? What was it like to catch glimpses of God?

Do you remember a time before you believed? How was God working in your life then?

How did God gently plant the first seed of faith in your heart?

What was your soul's response to God's initial invitation?

## Reflection

Nothing is wasted in God's economy. He is present in every situation, using each experience to help us along the spiritual path. Consider this passage as you reflect on the first stirrings of faith in your life:

> *As the rain and the snow come down from heaven,*
> *and do not return to it without watering the earth*
> *and making it bud and flourish ...*
> *so is my word that goes out from my mouth:*
> *It will not return to me empty,*
> *but will accomplish what I desire*
> *and achieve the purpose for which I sent it.*
> *Isaiah 55:10-11 (NIV)*

How did God accomplish his purpose through your early spiritual experiences?

What other thoughts do you have about awakening?

## A Special Prayer

Jesus—it's taken a while but I'm finally waking up. I didn't even know you were with me while I slept, but you stayed by my side anyway. Thank you for gently planting the seeds of faith in my soul. Keep my heart in joyful anticipation of your awakenings that are new every morning. Amen.

# CHAPTER 4

# *Earning*

*We remember before our God and Father*
*your work produced by faith,*
*your labor prompted by love,*
*and your endurance inspired by hope*
*in our Lord Jesus Christ.*
*1 Thessalonians 1:3 (NIV)*

Do you want your life to matter? Do you long to feel important to those closest to you? The heart of every human aches to be remembered and valued. We're on the lookout for ways to build a life of significance, hoping to be loved and admired.

When we're ignored, we intensify our search. What will it take to be noticed? Is it success? Beauty? Athletics? Whatever the endeavor, we're determined to shine. Surely that's how we'll get the attention and affection we crave. Or is it?

## My Story

When I was a child, the message rang loud and clear. "When you have accomplished enough, then we will love you."

No one ever spoke it, but I knew it was true. Where was the key to earning my family's affection? I finally found it in playing the violin.

After years of study, I stepped up the pace in high school. I was determined to practice eight hours every day. But homework and housework kept getting in the way. Since my bedroom had a door to the outside, I decided to leave it open every night, even in the dead of winter. By 4:00 a.m., my room was so cold that I had to get up and practice.

I worked hard, often without a teacher. Eventually all those exhausting hours began to pay off. I was accepted to a prestigious music conservatory in Boston. But, to my dismay, I felt like a fish out of water. I was there for the wrong reason—to earn love—and it didn't work. When I finally gave up the violin years later, scarcely anyone noticed. The mission had failed and my hope of love and acceptance evaporated.

## Encouragement

Often our efforts just aren't enough to earn the love we seek. No matter how hard we try, others can and will let us down. In the end, a non-stop string of pursuits can leave us feeling as hollow as an empty coffee can.

God is the only one to whom we are always important. We're first in his book, every second of every day. We don't have to earn his favor. We're made in his image, and he loves us with an everlasting love. Although he delights in our talents, he adores us for who we are.

## Your Story

When have you felt unimportant or unloved by others?

How did you try to earn their affection?

In looking back, how do you understand that situation now?

How have you sensed God's presence in your struggle for significance?

## Reflection

We can work incredibly hard to earn someone's love. We sacrifice everything just to be important in the eyes of those we care about. Could our priorities be misplaced? Prayerfully ponder this verse:

> *"Do not work for food that spoils,*
> *but for food that endures to eternal life,*
> *which the Son of Man will give you.*
> *For on him God the Father has placed his seal of approval."*
> *John 6:27 (NIV)*

If you didn't work for "food that spoils," how would your life be different?

What other thoughts do you have about earning approval?

## A Special Prayer

Jesus—I've spent so much time trying to earn my way to love and success. It hasn't worked very well. I've forgotten that you are always with me, whether my life is filled with triumph or despair. Help me to remember that I am eternally yours, regardless of fame or fortune. Hold me close forever. Amen.

CHAPTER 5

# Belonging

*"My relatives stay far away,*
*and my friends have turned against me.*
*My family is gone,*
*and my close friends have forgotten me."*
*Job 19:13-14 (NLT)*

Do you long to feel connected? Perhaps you're looking for nurturing and acceptance from your family. Or you yearn for closer relationships with friends. Is your heart searching for a life-long mate? The need to belong is a deeply human desire.

A lucky few of us feel a sense of community from the very beginning of our lives. We know we are loved and cherished. But for many, it is an elusive dream, a fantasy that seems forever out of reach. For some, it's hard to even remember a single time when we experienced that kind of affection.

## My Story

Deep inside I always knew I didn't belong. My family wasn't much into connectedness. We didn't share many evening meals together at home. In fact, the children and adults ate separately. The big exceptions were birthdays and holidays. With the video camera running, we tried to look like the perfect family.

I could count on one hand the number of times my family watched a movie together. Vacations were just as rare. Shopping trips for clothes—or anything else—barely made the radar screen. Even a mother-daughter outing to buy a prom dress was merely a chore to be finished as soon as possible.

Although I had a few friends as a child, I usually felt like an outsider on the playground. It didn't get much better in high school. I was uneasy at parties and only went to one sporting event. I had no idea how to connect, fit in, or have a relationship.

## Encouragement

Many of us yearn to find our special place in the world—a place where we belong and all is safe and warm. When we are denied that sense of connectedness, our need only grows stronger. We desperately search for a human bond, but don't have a clue how to find it.

Why do we forget the one special relationship that always meets our needs? Someone is there who never forgets us. He has our names engraved on the palm of his hand. With God, we're never "missing in action." He knows exactly where we are, every minute of the day.

## Your Story

Describe a time you felt like you didn't belong.

How did you cope with the situation?

In what ways did the experience affect you later in life?

How do you perceive God's purpose in that time of disconnection?

## Reflection

The search for belonging is the theme song of many lives. But there is a different tune we can play. As you ponder this passage, consider the possibility that you are never truly alone. There is someone who always knows your name.

> *For none of us lives for ourselves alone,*
> *and none of us dies for ourselves alone.*
> *If we live, we live for the Lord;*
> *and if we die, we die for the Lord.*
> *So, whether we live or die, we belong to the Lord.*
> *Romans 14:7-8 (NIV)*

How does it feel to know the Lord calls you his own, no matter what?

What other thoughts do you have about belonging to God?

## A Special Prayer

Jesus—sometimes I feel so alone and rejected. Often there seems to be no hope. And yet I know I am yours, and you wait eagerly to see me every single day. Help me to know I belong to you always—that you love me with an everlasting love. Show me my own special place in your grand design. Amen.

# CHAPTER 6

# *Judging*

*Why do you judge your brother or sister?*
*Or why do you treat them with contempt?*
*For we will all stand before God's judgment seat.*
Romans 14:10 (NIV)

Judging others can be so much fun. It's a pastime that offers endless amusement. It can be a team sport or a solo act. We can condemn and lecture people in person, or we can snicker behind their backs. Either way, we're one up, and they're one down—and we like it that way.

Often, we judge others to show we're better. Other times, we just want to believe we're right. But does putting another person down really prove anything? Labeling someone as less doesn't make us more. And, ultimately, only God knows the real truth.

## My Story

My parents didn't like Christians, so neither did I. Our family's slogan was, "Christians are dumb, stupid, weak, and can't take care of themselves." We believed Jesus was just a crutch for those people—something they weren't strong enough to live without.

My exposure to Christianity was minimal, mostly from playing the violin at my friends' churches. I always felt so sorry for the people in the congregation. Why didn't they know any better? What in the world did they need God for?

I figured it was understandable for a woman to be in church. After all, women have been considered the weaker sex for centuries. But what about the men? They ought to be stronger than that! I secretly believed everyone should be a smart, independent thinker—like me.

## Encouragement

We don't see things as God sees them. How could we? Our minds are too limited. And it isn't our place to judge anyway. Only God sees into our hearts and the hearts of those we condemn. He alone knows the motives, hurts, and fears that drive each of us.

When we judge others, we often end up being wrong. Maybe that's because we're blind to our own faults and challenges. In God's perspective, we're all created in his image, but he's the only one qualified to judge. Yet it's so tempting, even as he gently holds us back from our critical ways, to break loose, run forward, and judge again.

## Your Story

Describe a time when you judged someone.

What challenges were you facing that influenced you to judge this person?

In looking back, was your judgment right or wrong? In what ways?

How do you think God would have preferred you to handle the situation?

## Reflection

In the end, all of us must stand and explain ourselves to God. He says if we judge, we will be judged, and if we forgive, we will be forgiven. Prayerfully consider this passage:

> *Let the Lord judge the peoples.*
> *Vindicate me, LORD, according to my righteousness,*
> *according to my integrity, O Most High.*
> *Psalm 7:8 (NIV)*

When God searches your mind and heart, what will he find?

What additional thoughts do you have about judging others?

## A Special Prayer

Jesus—I struggle so with judging. It feels fun and amusing when I'm talking with friends about the shortcomings of others. But later I regret it and wish I could take back those words. Help me to keep watch over my heart and my mouth. I want to stay out of the judgment business and let you do the job only you can do. Amen.

# CHAPTER 7

# *Striving*

*What do people get in this life
for all their hard work and anxiety?
Their days of labor are filled with pain and grief;
even at night their minds cannot rest.*
Ecclesiastes 2:22-23a (NLT)

Will we ever have enough? Will we ever be enough? For many of us, something is always missing in our lives. Maybe it's recognition. Maybe it's money. Maybe it's acceptance. Whatever "it" is, we feel incomplete, so we spend our lives chasing after it.

There are so many ways to play the "good enough" game. Most of them involve striving to do better, be greater, or have more. We're like an athlete always trying to clear the Olympic high jump, but someone keeps raising that pesky bar. We keep practicing and improving, but we never quite make it.

❧   ❧   ❧   ❧   ❧   ❧   ❧

## My Story

In my soul, I believed professional success was the key to getting what I wanted out of life. Everything would magically be okay if I just performed well enough. Then I would get the "cosmic phone call" from my family and friends, affirming that I had passed the test. Dreams of deep and lasting relationships would be fulfilled and I would be loved.

Eagerly, I jumped onto the treadmill of accomplishment at an early age. As the years passed, I expanded into bigger and better performances, graduating at the top of my college class, becoming a CPA, and owning a flourishing accounting practice. Being a good mom was a definite priority, even during stints as a professional musician, college instructor, community leader, and radio talk show host.

But the cosmic phone call never came. No matter how hard I tried, love and acceptance remained elusive. I felt rejected, insignificant, and empty. The magic treadmill got me nowhere.

## Encouragement

Striving is an American pastime. All we need is the next promotion, a little more money, a beautiful spouse, and perfect children. Then our lives will be wonderful and satisfying. Or will they? No matter how much we accomplish, true happiness lingers just beyond our reach.

During these years of striving, God knocks at the door, hoping for a moment of our time. Sadly, in our drive to achieve, we close our eyes to his request. We want to make it on our own. We want to be good enough. So, the one who cares for us unconditionally for all eternity remains patiently outside, his loving invitation unanswered.

## Your Story

What have you striven for? Was it wealth, success, love, or something else?

What pain did you hope to heal?

Where was Jesus during your "good enough" game?

What truth has God revealed to you about striving?

## Reflection

Even a lifetime of accomplishment, with all its glitter and success, leaves us empty-handed in the end. Sit for a moment and reflect on this passage from Scripture:

> *"Give careful thought to your ways.*
> *You have planted much, but have harvested little.*
> *You eat, but never have enough.*
> *You drink, but never have your fill.*
> *You put on clothes, but are not warm.*
> *You earn wages, only to put them in a purse with holes in it."*
> *Haggai 1:5b-6 (NIV)*

What would it take for you to be content with God?

What other thoughts do you have about striving?

## A Special Prayer

Jesus—forgive me. I'm so busy trying to be good enough that I fail to see you in my life. The messages of love you gently whisper in my ear are drowned out. Help me rest in your arms and know you have loved me from the beginning of time. In your eyes, I've always been accepted and enough. Amen.

# CHAPTER 8

# *Turning*

*Return to the LORD your God,
for he is gracious and compassionate,
slow to anger and abounding in love.*
*Joel 2:13b (NIV)*

Have you ever been inside a building and lost your sense of direction? Which way is north? Where is the parking lot? How do you find the exit? Sometimes life is like that. We get so caught up in the maze of our own circumstances that we can't see the way out.

Maybe we need to turn around and try a completely different direction. That's easier said than done, especially when the route we're walking feels familiar and safe. But then a crisis stops us in our tracks. Suddenly, we realize something is terribly wrong. It's time to change—now!

ço  ço  ço  ço  ço  ço  ço

## My Story

The pregnancy test was positive, but this baby wasn't planned. My husband thought he was too old for another child and asked me to consider an abortion. Although I said no, a couple months later I had a miscarriage. Problem solved—from his point of view. But I kept thinking, "There's something wrong here." The loss caused me to take a long, hard look at my life. I didn't like what I saw.

On the outside, I looked successful. By the world's standards, I certainly *was* successful. But reality told a different story. I had a distant and detached marriage, no real friends, and was a workaholic. I was a robot on autopilot, a slave to my overheated calendar.

For years, I had closed my eyes to the situation. I figured if I kept busy enough, I could ignore it. Eventually, however, I became so exhausted from overwork that I could barely get up off the floor. A serious course correction was looming ahead.

## Encouragement

Turning to God is never easy, especially when we're busy looking in the opposite direction. Which way should we go? Where can we find peace? Maybe we don't even know what we're looking for. Eventually, all sense of direction fails and we end up wandering in the mist, crying for help.

But perhaps all we need to do is move an inch. It's like rock climbing. If we reach up, reposition our feet, and shift our weight a little, our perspective changes. Suddenly we can see God beside us, gracious and loving as always.

## Your Story

When have you found yourself facing the wrong way, unsure where to go next?

What were some challenges that kept you stuck?

In what ways did you start to turn around?

How did you see God helping you walk toward him?

## Reflection

Sometimes change feels like making a U-turn in a semi-truck with no power steering—a huge, exhausting challenge. But when it's done, you're pointed in the right direction. Then all you really need is to know that God is with you. Ponder this passage for a moment:

> *Turn to me and have mercy,*
> *for I am alone and in deep distress.*
> *My problems go from bad to worse.*
> *Oh, save me from them all!*
> *Psalm 25:16-17 (NLT)*

In the trials of life, how do you sense God moving toward you in compassion and grace?

What other thoughts do you have about turning to God?

## A Special Prayer

Jesus—I'm struggling. My life is full of chaos and trouble. Which way should I turn? Where is my help? Please pick me up and set me back on the path that leads only to you. Lead me by the hand and protect me. Be my rock and refuge forever and ever. Amen.

# CHAPTER 9

# *Searching*

*"You will seek me and find me
when you seek me with all your heart.
I will be found by you," declares the LORD,
"and will bring you back from captivity."*
*Jeremiah 29:13-14a (NIV)*

Most of us would agree that what is lost should be found.
But what if we don't even realize it's lost? Perhaps we just
have a vague feeling inside that something is missing. There's
obviously a hole, but we have no idea what should fill it.

Often we find the missing piece by trial and error. We try
one pursuit, and the door closes. We go to another door and
the latch is locked tight. We keep turning knobs until one
miraculously releases. Hesitantly, we step into a room we've
never seen before.

❧  ❧  ❧  ❧  ❧  ❧  ❧

## My Story

Something was missing. My heart was empty, and I didn't know why. There had to be a solution so I started searching. I read every self-help book I could get my hands on. I exercised. I baked bread. I even watched Lawrence Welk re-runs. But nothing worked. I couldn't find the answer. So, I doubled down on my quest.

Intrigued with New Age practices, I sat every night in a darkened room facing a small electric light. I would meditate on the universe, pretending to bask in its glow. Then I took up affirmations and repeated encouraging phrases to myself. I even recorded them, hoping to penetrate my subconscious while brushing my teeth. No matter what I did, the stubborn hole remained.

One day, I came across a book by Norman Vincent Peale that spoke to my heart. The short excerpts and quotes he included attracted me, so I made them into flashcards and read them every day. It didn't occur to me that they were from the Bible. I only cared that they gave me peace.

❧  ❧  ❧  ❧  ❧  ❧  ❧

## Encouragement

Sometimes we have no idea what we're looking for. All we know is we need something new. So the hunt begins. Some of us search in books. Others look to healthy living. Many turn to movies and television. If we're truly seeking to fill the emptiness, in the end we will be looking for God.

Still, the search for him can be like driving through a dense fog. Even with our headlights on, we see only a few feet ahead. Yet with every mile we travel, the road ahead gets a little clearer. Eventually the fog lifts, and we spot Jesus waiting just around the bend.

## Your Story

Describe a time you realized something was missing in your life.

How did you search for it?

In what ways did your life change as a result?

How did God guide you along the way?

## Reflection

Sometimes our search can seem endless, with no guarantee that we'll find what we're looking for. But that isn't true. This famous passage promises we will find what we are seeking. Reflect on its message to you.

> *"Ask and it will be given to you;*
> *seek and you will find;*
> *knock and the door will be opened to you.*
> *For everyone who asks receives; the one who seeks finds;*
> *and to the one who knocks, the door will be opened.*
> *Matthew 7:7-8 (NIV)*

How does this verse speak to you about your spiritual journey?

What other thoughts do you have about searching?

## A Special Prayer

Jesus—where are you? I know you are nearby, encouraging me to come to you. But sometimes you seem shrouded in the mistiness of my eyes. Clear my vision, so I can find the path to run into your arms. Replace my struggle with the peace only you can give—the peace that passes all understanding. Amen.

# CHAPTER 10

# *Encountering*

*My soul thirsts for God, for the living God.*
*When can I go and meet with God?*
*Psalm 42:2 (NIV)*

Our anxious eyes survey the landscape. We're looking for something—something bigger than ourselves, something more powerful, something or someone with the answers we seek. Let's face it—what we really want is an encounter with God. But where is he?

Trying to find him can be like wandering alone in the desert. Where should we turn? There are no landmarks. If we truly desire to see Jesus, we may need a little help. Perhaps a guiding hand can open our eyes. But what if the person or situation catches us by surprise? Will our souls be receptive?

## My Story

The public meeting was packed with loud, angry citizens, fuming about the local bus service. As a newly elected city council member, I did my best to cope with the chaos. Through the commotion, I heard the mayor call a recess to cool the meeting down.

During the break, I burst into his office. "This is such a mess. What are we going to do?" I cried, waving my arms excitedly. He pointed me to a chair and said, "You need to relax. I'm going to give you some Bible verses. Go home tonight and read them." He rattled off a list of verse numbers. Knowing better than to offend the mayor, I grabbed a yellow sticky pad and scribbled them down. But what in the world was Philippians?

That night, I borrowed a Bible and read every verse. I was enthralled. Here was the answer I was searching for. Every evening afterward, I locked myself in the bathroom—the only place where mothers have any real privacy. Pulling the Bible out from the cabinet under the sink, I faithfully read a little bit each night. Even though I didn't understand most of it, I made it all the way from Matthew to Revelation.

## Encouragement

Our spiritual guides may not realize how they impact our lives. Perhaps they have had many similar conversations in the past. Maybe they have never spoken openly of their faith before. It doesn't matter. What is important is how we respond. Will our eyes be opened by a word or a phrase? Will we see God?

When we truly encounter God, we know it's him. Somehow, we're compelled to walk toward him. We're drawn in by his irresistible force. Whether our spiritual guide continues with us or steps back after the first encounter, the direction of our journey is changed forever.

## Your Story

Have you had a surprising encounter with Christ, either on your own or through another person? What was it like?

Why do you suppose this special circumstance or person appeared in your path?

Were you open to the situation, or did you run and hide? Why?

In what ways do you sense that God arranged this encounter just for you?

## Reflection

In our search for God, we may find him in unusual places, speaking through unexpected people. But if we search, we will find him. Consider your own life as you prayerfully reflect on this verse:

> *If you search for [God] with all your heart and soul,*
> *you will find him.*
> *Deuteronomy 4:29b (NLT)*

What does it take for you to truly know God?

What other thoughts do you have about encountering God?

## A Special Prayer

Jesus—where are you? I know you're out there! But I may need a little help finding you. Please send over a guide for me, someone I can trust who will lead me to you. As this person gently points me in the right direction, help me to be receptive. In the end, I know I'll find what I'm looking for—you! Amen.

# CHAPTER 11

# Exploring

*I searched everywhere, determined to find wisdom
and to understand the reason for things.*
Ecclesiastes 7:25a (NLT)

There is so much to explore in Christianity. Where do we start? If you were raised in the church, you may have the basic building blocks of faith already in place. If the Christian life is new to you, you're probably starting from scratch. That's OK—every journey begins somewhere.

Christianity is pretty simple. Christ died for our sins. And yet, in reality, there is so much more. It's a whole belief system wrapped in an intricate tapestry of stories, letters, and truths about what it is to be human in relationship with a holy God. It takes a lifetime to explore all of his promises.

## My Story

It was that special autumn day when everybody gets an extra hour. I decided to use mine to check out a Christian church. But where would I go? I looked in the phone book, but there were literally hundreds of choices. Finally, I spied an ad for a big downtown church. Ah-ha!

During my run for city council I had sent out lots of campaign letters, even to people I didn't know. The pastor of this church was one of them. Though most folks just throw away mail from politicians, he had sent a gracious reply. That's why I decided to visit his church that morning.

My seven-year-old daughter and I silently slinked into the back row and hoped nobody would recognize us. But something was missing from the service that day. It was the sermon. Instead of preaching, the pastor asked several people to stand up and tell about how Jesus had changed their lives and what the church meant to them. Hearing their stories, I knew they had something I wanted.

## Encouragement

It takes guts to set out on an exploration. We must go to unfamiliar places. Often we end up in situations that leave us feeling awkward or uneasy. Yet new discoveries energize us as our understanding deepens. God uses each opportunity to draw us closer to himself. He is always reaching out.

For some, our first experience of him is in church. For others it can be on a mountain, by the sea, or even in front of the television. Regardless of the context, God extends an invitation to explore. Wherever we start, the road leading to Christ lies open before us.

## Your Story

How did you initially begin to explore Christianity?

Was it confusing, or did all the details fall into place?

What were some difficult parts of your exploration?

How did you sense God leading you to himself?

## Reflection

When our eyes are first opened and we gingerly take our initial baby steps to explore the faith, we don't realize how eager God is to bring us into his fold. Pray and listen as this passage speaks to you:

> *I myself will tend my sheep*
> *and give them a place to lie down in peace,*
> *says the Sovereign LORD.*
> *I will search for my lost ones who strayed away,*
> *and I will bring them safely home again.*
> *I will bandage up the injured and strengthen the weak.*
> *Ezekiel 34:15-16a (NLT)*

How is God personally guiding you to a deeper discovery of the faith?

What other thoughts do you have about exploring?

## A Special Prayer

Jesus—you never stopped searching for me until you found me. I know your heart cries out when even one of your sheep is lost. Please hold me safe as I explore life with you and the wonderful promises you have for me. I have so much to learn and experience as you draw me ever closer. Amen.

# CHAPTER 12

# *Pursuing*

*Pursue righteousness and a godly life,
along with faith, love, perseverance, and gentleness.*
*1 Timothy 6:11b (NLT)*

We want it. We've got to have it. Nothing, absolutely nothing, can stand in the way of our relentless pursuit. Perhaps it's a possession. Maybe it's an experience. It could be a relationship. All we know is we can't rest until it's ours.

Pursuing God is a little like peeking in the door of an ice cream shop. The bright lights and sweet aromas draw us in. We're mesmerized by all the flavors and eagerly request a sample. Even if we were just innocently passing by, now we've got to have that cone. So it is with God. One taste, and we're hooked.

## My Story

After my first Sunday in church, I knew I had to go back. My husband and son weren't interested, but my little girl liked to go. The next weekend, there we were in our back-row seats again. Although it would take some time and courage for us to move to a seat nearer the front, we never missed a Sunday.

Then I discovered the Wednesday night classes. They looked fairly painless and non-threatening, and it didn't hurt that the church served dinner before each session. One less meal to cook! I began to scour the Sunday bulletin for cool classes.

Later I was invited to join a new Bible study. This wasn't any ordinary, run-of-the-mill group. It was a traveling dinner party, complete with an occasional sleepover. The leader suggested a fill-in-the-blank study book. I came to the first meeting expecting to wing it and was amazed that the other women had actually written the answers in their books. Quickly, I shaped up and followed suit.

## Encouragement

The pursuit of God is unlike any trip we've ever taken. It's not like going to the store to buy new shoes or a blender. Once we get a glimpse of him, we can't let go. We leave no opportunity untouched. After all, the stakes are huge. We're talking about the God of the universe.

We tend to forget, though, that Jesus is pursuing us just as passionately. We may think we're chasing after him, but that's only half the story. In reality, he was hot on our trail before we ever even heard his name.

## Your Story

Have you felt a desire to pursue God? Describe how and when.

What opportunities did God put in your path so you could find him?

Describe the challenges you faced as you pursued Jesus.

How did you perceive God's presence guiding you in this journey?

## Reflection

As we seek to know God and experience his presence, we come to realize we're made in his image and are part of his wonderful design. Think about this as you reflect on the verse below:

> *"Listen to me, all who hope for deliverance —*
> *all who seek the LORD!*
> *Consider the rock from which you were cut,*
> *the quarry from which you were mined."*
> *Isaiah 51:1 (NLT)*

As you pursue God, how do you see his image reflected in you?

What other thoughts do you have about pursuing God?

## A Special Prayer

Jesus—there are so many places to find you. It's like you're everywhere! And so you are. Thank you for planting the seed of faith in my heart. Keep my feet on the path that leads only to you. Help me pursue you with all my strength, all my heart, and all my soul. Amen.

# CHAPTER 13

# *Committing*

*Into your hands I commit my spirit;*
*deliver me, LORD, my faithful God.*
*Psalm 31:5 (NIV)*

Whom do you trust? In what do you put your faith? These
days, we have so many options. In today's society, even a
decision as momentous as choosing a religious faith can seem
almost on par with picking a breakfast cereal. Why commit
ourselves to God, the Bible, or anything Christian, when we
could just as easily believe whatever feels good at the time?

Commitment is a tough sell these days. Sure, we want
loyalty, steadfastness, and devotion—from everyone else. But
what about ourselves? Are we ready to give up all our options
to settle on just one? Too often, it feels safer to keep a few other
choices in our back pocket. That way, we'll never be stuck.

## My Story

I was considering joining the church, so I went to the new member class. The leader dutifully covered all the important tenets of the faith. As I listened, my uneasiness grew.

Could I actually accept Christianity? Most of it sounded reasonable enough, but some points seemed so narrow-minded. My old anti-Christian mind rebelled. I wanted to believe the parts I liked and ignore the rest. I didn't realize how the major threads of Christianity all weave together. If I pulled out a few strands, I would end up with an unraveled tapestry—not a changed life.

After a few months, I noticed that the pastor prayed a special prayer at the end of every service. He said there might be people there—like me—who hadn't made up their minds yet about Jesus. He urged each one to pray silently with him and commit themselves to Christ. Finally, one Sunday I cast my doubts aside and prayed right along with him.

## Encouragement

Faith means committing to something we can't see. It's about letting go and believing. Ultimately, we must come to grips with the idea of abandoning ourselves to God—not the God we made up or the God we feel comfortable with, but the God of the universe. Will we do it?

We can meander all day on the wide road of spiritual experimentation. Still, at sunset we find only a dead end. In the distance we can see Jesus, standing at the narrow gate, beckoning us to him. The opening is small and hard to pass through. Yet a golden vista of life awaits us on the other side.

## Your Story

Where are you in the process of your commitment to Christ?

How did you get to this point?

What lingering doubts have troubled you?

How has God guided you through this experience?

## Reflection

Committing is never easy. For some, it can seem as scary as swinging through the air on a trapeze without a net. Is God really there? Will he catch us? Contemplate these questions while you ponder this passage:

> *God has come to save me.*
> *I will trust in him and not be afraid.*
> *The LORD GOD is my strength and my song;*
> *he has given me victory.*
> *Isaiah 12:2 (NLT)*

As you've considered pledging your life to Christ, how has your trust deepened?

What other thoughts do you have about committing?

## A Special Prayer

Jesus—I want to keep walking your special path. But the world has so many choices and sometimes I don't know which way to go. Help me grow in my commitment to you. As you enfold me in your arms, let me know I am safe and all is well. Give me the courage to follow you and to trust you always. Amen.

# CHAPTER 14

# *Healing*

*He has not ignored or belittled the suffering of the needy.*
*He has not turned his back on them,*
*but has listened to their cries for help.*
*Psalm 22:24 (NLT)*

Sometimes life just hurts. Much as we long for simple, joyous days, pain breaks in. Our hearts ache over past wounds. Today's sorrow consumes us. Where is the miracle cure—the one that erases all the anguish?

As desperately as we want to heal, we don't know how. The search is on for a simple, permanent solution. We wish we could scoop all the pain out of our hearts, like hollowing out a pumpkin. Or perhaps we could let the hurt drain from our souls into a cosmic sink, never to be felt again.

## My Story

Sitting in a small office, I stared at the checklist on the desk. How on earth did I end up at the Domestic Violence Center? Having been divorced, I was now in a new relationship. Surely things couldn't be this bad! As I finished checking all the boxes that described what had happened, a dark truth flooded my soul. The abuse was real.

Clearly, I stood at a crossroad and had to change something—now! Slowly and painfully, I made yet another U-turn. Completing the educational programs at the center, I began working with a counselor and made a serious commitment to my devotional life.

At the same time, I joined a twelve-step program for those affected by other people's drinking. As usual, I jumped right in, got a sponsor, and began learning the steps. During the next five years, my life turned around once again as I came to a deeper understanding of God and myself.

## Encouragement

In our quest for wholeness, we ultimately find ourselves in partnership with God. He is the great physician who restores our health. Yet if we don't participate, we're like a patient refusing treatment. He longs to stitch up the broken and torn pieces of our lives, but he won't if we keep squirming around on his operating table.

If we want to heal, we must accept the cure. It may mean saying goodbye to old ways that only hurt us. It may mean turning to walk in a new direction. It may mean humbly accepting help from others. When God holds out the spoon, it's a good idea to swallow the medicine.

## Your Story

Describe a pivotal turning point in your life.

What steps did you take to work through the pain and change your life?

How did you overcome the obstacles to healing?

In what ways did you sense God's presence and compassion in your suffering?

## Reflection

Sometimes it's hard to face another day as we peer out from under our blanket of pain. Still, God is with us, always holding us, never letting us go. Consider your own struggles as you pray about this passage:

> *Remember your promise to me; it is my only hope.*
> *Your promise revives me;*
> *it comforts me in all my troubles.*
> *Psalm 119:49-50 (NLT)*

How does God comfort you through his promise of hope, even in the midst of difficulties?

What other thoughts do you have about healing?

## A Special Prayer

Jesus—as I've faced the anguish and pain of life, you've always been with me. Even in my darkest days, you were right there, offering encouragement and hope. Help me put aside the aches of yesterday as together we walk the road of true healing—the healing only you can offer. Amen.

# CHAPTER 15

# *Learning*

*Let us discern for ourselves what is right;*
*let us learn together what is good.*
Job 34:4 *(NIV)*

Going it alone is tough. We want to learn about God. We long to grow in our faith. But where do we start? Whom do we ask? It's like going on safari by ourselves. We're searching for lions, elephants, and giraffes, but we don't know where to find them. All we can do is scan the horizon, disappointed and bewildered.

Being a new disciple of Christ is never easy, and doing it single-handedly is even harder. We're filled with joy and excitement at finding Jesus, but now what? Navigating the terrain isn't easy. We stumble on rocks. We can't read the map. Where is our safari guide?

## My Story

Knowing I needed help, I signed up for the women's mentoring program at church. Everyone told me how lucky I was to be assigned to a woman who had traveled the world in ministry and knew most of the Bible by heart.

My new spiritual guide didn't want to just chit-chat and trade recipes. She wouldn't waste her time unless her "trainee" did a weekly Bible lesson with her. We launched into study after study. Years went by, and we kept going. One day her husband told me, "We really like you because you always do your homework!"

This special relationship put me on a fast track to growing in faith. The life lessons were many. Whether we were studying scripture, solving problems, or just being friends, having a spiritual guide shaped my Christian journey in a profound way. It gave me confidence and a sure footing to follow Jesus more deeply.

## Encouragement

Let's face it. Going it alone as a new Christian doesn't work very well. Re-inventing the wheel is inefficient at best. Why dabble in "trial and error" faith when spiritual guides are ready and willing to help? We can double our progress by following the lead of those who have traveled this path before.

Jesus never intended us to be loners. Just as he encouraged little children to sit with him, he entrusts younger believers into the wise and compassionate care of those who have walked with him for years. Holding hands with a sure-footed guide brings us deeper into the warmth of God's love and grace.

## Your Story

Have you had a spiritual guide or special group of friends that made a difference in your life? Please describe them.

What qualities of this person or group were particularly helpful?

In what ways were you led deeper into the faith?

How did you perceive God's hand at work in this relationship?

## Reflection

When we walk with another in faith, we learn about God together. Jesus has so much to teach us through a guiding friendship. How might these words from the Apostle Paul apply to your life?

> *Whatever you have learned or received or heard from me,*
> *or seen in me—put it into practice.*
> *And the God of peace will be with you.*
> *Philippians 4:9 (NIV)*

When you've heard Christ speaking through others, how has this brought you peace?



What other thoughts do you have about learning?



## A Special Prayer

Jesus—going it alone doesn't work very well, especially for me. I need some help! Please set a special guide in my path, someone who has as much to teach as I have to learn. Give me a receptive heart as I learn what it means to walk with you every day. Amen.

# CHAPTER 16

# *Listening*

*Joyful are those who listen to me,*
*watching for me daily at my gates,*
*waiting for me outside my home!*
*For whoever finds me finds life*
*and receives favor from the LORD.*
Proverbs 8:34-35 (NLT)

Do we listen to God—really listen? When someone asks what the Lord is telling us these days, do we have a good answer? Or do we just mumble a few niceties and quickly change the subject?

There are many reasons we don't always listen to God. Some of us are too busy to slow down and sit with him. Others fear what he might say, and tune him out. Many don't recall ever hearing his voice and haven't a clue how to start.

## My Story

Even before I knew Jesus, he had spoken to me. One day, while cleaning the bathroom, I sensed an unmistakable voice. As I pulled the shower curtain closed, the voice said he had plans for me. "Wow! What was that all about?" I felt astonished and bewildered.

Years later, as my faith grew, I began writing down what he said. My collection of little hand-written scraps of paper multiplied, as did my computer files when I started typing his words. His tone was wise, encouraging, and sometimes even funny. The voice was always the same—the one I had come to know and trust.

Even with such a promising start, listening was still a struggle. Often I was busy and didn't discipline myself to stop and pay attention. Weeks or months would go by, and I only listened for his voice as I drifted off to sleep.

## Encouragement

Let's ask again—are we really listening to what God has to say? Chances are he's tried to speak with us, but we make it difficult to hear him. Sometimes we do all the talking during our prayer time, and he doesn't get a word in edgewise. Other times we ignore him entirely because we're consumed by the busyness of our lives. Relationships without a two-way conversation don't grow and strengthen.

Fortunately for us, Jesus is patient. He keeps ringing our doorbell, hoping we'll unlock the latch and let him in. He has so much to tell us—words of comfort and wisdom. Yet with our multi-media world bombarding us daily, it's often hard to hear him over all the racket.

## Your Story

Have you ever sensed God speaking to you? Can you describe that time with him?

Did you listen or ignore him, hoping he would go away?

How did you feel about hearing God's voice?

What could you have done to be a better listener?

## Reflection

God wants more than a one-way relationship with us. Because we are so precious to him, he longs for us to recognize his voice every single time he speaks. Consider what he might be saying to you in this verse:

> *Whether you turn to the right or to the left,*
> *your ears will hear a voice behind you, saying,*
> *"This is the way; walk in it."*
> *Isaiah 30:21 (NIV)*

How do you feel, knowing God's voice will guide you wherever you go?

What other thoughts do you have about listening?

## A Special Prayer

Jesus—I'm listening. I truly am, even though it may not look like it! I want to hear when you call. But I need a little help to clearly perceive your voice. Give me the discipline to set aside the all the cares and noises of the day and focus on your words. Amen.

# CHAPTER 17

# *Forsaking*

*'Leave your country and your people,' God said,*
*'and go to the land I will show you.'*
*Acts 7:3 (NIV)*

A radical devotion to Christ—being at one with him—demands purity of heart. For most of us, our lives miss the mark by a mile. Perhaps we hold onto bad habits. Maybe our relationships don't honor Jesus. Either way, the time will come when we are called to leave behind the things of the past and walk in faith toward God.

Forsaking our old ways can be a double-edged sword. Sure, we understand our lives will change for the better as we follow Christ. Still, leaving the old behind and walking toward the new can be a lonely road. If we must venture away from life as we know it, we need God's tender hand to hold.

ဆုံ   ဆုံ   ဆုံ   ဆုံ   ဆုံ   ဆုံ   ဆုံ

## My Story

As I moved closer to God, parts of my life didn't click anymore. Change was on the horizon, but I felt resistant. I especially cherished my pre-Christian independence. It seemed like I could accomplish so much more when I was in charge of my own life. Although I knew it was important, waiting on God's direction felt slow and constricting.

I had to take an honest look at the freedom I cherished so deeply. Although my lifestyle was never especially wild, I did accept the world's standards as right and true. So I usually did whatever I wanted. But as my faith grew, I saw that life with Christ offered a different paradigm.

Unexpected changes in my close relationships proved to be a challenge. Some family members and friends couldn't connect with my new life at all. Even an innocent reference to Christianity seemed taboo. I realized they walked a path very different from mine. How long could we walk together?

## Encouragement

Letting go is never easy. Long held habits and thought patterns continue to intrude into our new lives. The possibility of an altered relationship with a loved one wrenches our very souls. Only the promise of a deepening connection with Jesus gives us the strength to do what he asks.

As we move closer to God and further from our old lives, he extends his hand to us. He gently helps us to safely cross the streams of difficulties that lie before us. He lifts us in his arms to protect and shield us, showing us the way.

## Your Story

As your relationship with God deepened, were there areas of your life he asked you to forsake?

How did you feel about his request?

What steps did you take to honor him in this?

In what ways did you see God's hand silently guiding you?

## Reflection

Ultimately, our job as Christians is to live for God. Even when our burdens feel impossibly difficult, we can remember the promise he has made. Ponder these words for a moment:

> *"Never will I leave you; never will I forsake you."*
> *So we say with confidence,*
> *"The Lord is my helper; I will not be afraid."*
> *Hebrews 13:5b-6a (NIV)*

In what ways might you feel comforted and strengthened by knowing Jesus will always be with you?

What other thoughts do you have about forsaking?

## A Special Prayer

Jesus—I know you'll never abandon me or leave me orphaned. But sometimes following you is challenging and even painful. Please stay with me as I struggle to pattern my life after yours. Help me rely on your promises and know you'll never, ever forsake me. Amen.

# CHAPTER 18

# Standing

*Whatever happens, conduct yourselves*
*in a manner worthy of the gospel of Christ.*
*Philippians 1:27a (NIV)*

Standing up for what is fair, just, and true is never easy. First we need to figure out what we believe. In a world where anything goes, this is no small task. Once we take a position, we must consider other questions. Where will we take our stand? When will we do it? How far should we go, and what's our strategy?

The real test comes when we run smack into other people's opinions, that are as strongly held as our own. No matter what we stand for, opposition is a given. How do we hold the line graciously, but firmly?

## My Story

During my years on city council, I saved tons of newspaper clippings. Whenever I was quoted, I stashed the article away in a cabinet. Years later, as I skimmed over the stories while carefully packing them away in a box, one theme caught my attention.

Over and over, the news accounts described me doing the same thing—standing up for what I felt was right. I would consider each issue carefully, look at every side, and then take a stand. I wasn't trying to be radical—just thoughtful and even-handed. Even when I was on the losing end of an eight to one vote, I could sleep at night knowing I had made my best judgment. God gave me the strength to stand.

As I sealed the box of clippings, I remembered an elderly gentleman who often attended city government meetings. Each time he spoke, he treated the council with kindness and respect. He invariably ended with the same advice: a leader always does the right thing. I never forgot him.

## Encouragement

In biblical times, the prophets took tough stands. They often faced brutal opposition for speaking truth that others couldn't or wouldn't see. But God was with them, whispering in their ears, walking with them every step of the way.

The great heroes and heroines of the faith knew how to stand for good. They understood the cost and willingly paid it. They protected themselves with the armor of God, who kept them safe as they continued to stand. He will do the same for us.

## Your Story

Describe a time when you took a difficult stand.

How did others oppose you?

What emotional and spiritual struggles did you endure?

How did you sense God's guiding hand helping you stand firm in your position?

## Reflection

Standing up for a cause is never easy. It is especially hard when you face condemnation from those you love. Yet God always has a reason for what he asks us to do. Let these words of scripture wash over your soul.

> *So, my dear brothers and sisters,*
> *be strong and immovable.*
> *Always work enthusiastically for the Lord,*
> *for you know that nothing you do*
> *for the Lord is ever useless.*
> *1 Corinthians 15:58 (NLT)*

How do you feel, knowing when God asks you to stand, it is for something that matters?

What other thoughts do you have about standing up for your beliefs?

## A Special Prayer

Jesus—sometimes taking a stand is tough. I want to do what is right but the winds of opposition threaten to blow me right over. I need your help. Please comfort me as I struggle. Hold my hand in adversity. Hide me under your wing as I suffer the inevitable hurts. In other words, be with me. Amen.

# CHAPTER 19

# *Obeying*

*"As the Father has loved me, so have I loved you.*
*Now remain in my love.*
*If you keep my commands, you will remain in my love,*
*just as I have kept my Father's commands*
*and remain in his love."*
*John 15:9-10 (NIV)*

"Do it, or else."

Ouch! That's not a pleasant way to be treated. Good thing God doesn't say it like that. But he does make sure we know exactly what he wants. He may even send a beautiful engraved invitation, requesting our obedience. Beneath the elegance, though, are a firm hand and an insistent voice.

What should we do? Are we to accept the invitation blindly, without even knowing the cost involved? Should we turn it down and go on with life as usual? Perhaps there's a middle ground. One thing is certain: in the end, God gets his way.

## My Story

My city council years were drawing to a close. Soon the term limits law would kick in, and I would have to give up my seat. What was next on the horizon? I could run for the legislature, but that meant living for months at a time in a different city. With a child still at home, it was out of the question.

There was always the mayor's job. Since the current mayor had the same term-limit date that I did, it seemed like a good opportunity. But when he decided to resign his office two years early, everything suddenly changed.

Instantly, I knew I wasn't supposed to run for mayor. While my city council colleagues hastily mounted their mayoral campaigns, God unmistakably nudged me toward seminary. I had no idea why he was calling me there. But I obediently followed and waited until the reason eventually emerged.

## Encouragement

Unquestioning obedience is scary. Are we truly hearing God's voice? How do we know what's in store for us? It would be so much easier if he would just play his hand, give us the facts, and show us the future.

We can always say no, and sometimes we do. But God is persistent and gently prods us a second or even third time. If we still don't answer, he may call someone else to the mission he had reserved for us. The cost of disobedience could be higher than if we had complied with his request in the first place.

## Your Story

Has God asked you to do something and you had no idea why? What were the circumstances?

How did you decide if you would obey his request?

Whether you obeyed him or not, how did you feel about it in the end?

In what ways did God strengthen your character through this?

## Reflection

Following God with a willing heart can be one of the hardest things we will ever do. Our new experience may be sunny and exciting or filled with pain. Either way, we walk with him in love. Prayerfully consider this passage as you reflect on your life of obedience:

> *Patient endurance is what you need now,*
> *so that you will continue to do God's will.*
> *Then you will receive all that he has promised.*
> *Hebrews 10:36 (NLT)*

What is the cost of ignoring God, versus the reward of obeying him?

What other thoughts do you have about obeying God?

## A Special Prayer

Jesus—help! I truly want to follow wherever you may lead. But I'm weak and sometimes just don't have the strength to obey. Please hold my hand and be my gentle guide as we move forward into whatever you have planned for us. I know it will be great in the end so let's get moving! Amen!

# CHAPTER 20

# *Growing*

*Grow in the grace and knowledge
of our Lord and Savior Jesus Christ.
To him be glory both now and forever! Amen.*

2 Peter 3:18 (NIV)

Staying home is comfy and safe. We have our routines.
Everything moves at a predictable pace. Nothing rattles us.
Nothing changes much. But as nice as that sounds, there's
a problem. Our humdrum reality can be stifling, our faith
merely skimming the surface.

Unless we step out of our comfort zones, we won't grow.
To deepen our faith, God sometimes calls us to explore
foreign territory. We don't recognize the signposts. Maybe
we can't even read the language. Danger could be lurking
around every corner. But we must push ahead.

## My Story

Gingerly, I opened the seminary door. Walking up the stairs felt overwhelming, yet strangely sweet. Most of my college experience had been at large universities, so the intimate atmosphere was enticing. Then the professor did something unexpected. He opened the class with a prayer. A sense of peace settled over me. I belonged there.

The actual coursework terrified me. After all, I was a relatively new Christian in a class full of pastors. The textbooks had all kinds of strange words I didn't know—like "exegesis." What in the world was that? On my first exam, I wrote a note to the professor: "Please be kind. I've only been a Christian for five years." He was.

Because I wasn't raised in the faith, I often felt at a disadvantage. It was a struggle to figure out how the Bible hung together. Just going to church every week wasn't enough. I needed "remedial theology." As I worked through the classes, a startling insight emerged: Christianity actually makes sense!

## Encouragement

Sound familiar? Sometimes we have to jump in, no matter how deep and cold the water. As we flounder around, a wonderful thing happens. God meets us there, scooping us out of the deep end and wrapping us in a fluffy towel.

He longs for us to make this journey. Until we grow and mature, we will always be infants, clamoring for attention. God's heart yearns for us to experience life as grown-up believers, ready and eager to receive all he has to offer.

## Your Story

When did you sense God pushing you into the deep waters of growth?

Where were you on your journey of spiritual development?

What struggles did you endure as you grew?

How did this experience shape your relationship with Christ?

## Reflection

The road to spiritual maturity is filled with uncertainty and fear, yet we are called to be courageous as we walk toward God. The special message of this passage strengthens us as we move ever closer to him.

> *Live a life worthy of the Lord*
> *and please him in every way:*
> *bearing fruit in every good work,*
> *growing in the knowledge of God,*
> *being strengthened with all power*
> *according to his glorious might.*
> *Colossians 1:10-11a (NIV)*

What changes do you see in your life as you grow in your knowledge of God?


What other thoughts do you have about growing in faith?


## A Special Prayer

Jesus—you continue to call my name, inviting me to meet you, but I'm afraid. I need courage! Please hold my hand as I move ahead in the scary and painful seasons of growth. It's time to step out and travel with you to new places, see new things, and gather new experiences. Amen.

# CHAPTER 21

# *Losing*

*If you cling to your life, you will lose it,*
*and if you let your life go, you will save it.*
Luke 17:33 (NLT)

What have you lost? The longer we live, the more likely we are to lose something that matters to us. Some of us are only lightly touched by loss. Others bear great sorrow through significant, gut-wrenching pain. Yet loss visits us all.

One of the hardest losses to bear is the rejection of a loved one. Perhaps that's because such a person knows us intimately, then chooses to be with us no longer. When we've revealed the depths of our souls to others, a parting of ways cuts to the core of our being.

ৡ৹ ৡ৹ ৡ৹ ৡ৹ ৡ৹ ৡ৹ ৡ৹

## My Story

Stunned, I stared at my computer screen in disbelief. After seven months of stony silence, the dreaded e-mail arrived. Dashing all hope of reconciliation, a close relative ended our relationship, severing a tie of more than 40 years. A wave of heartache washed over me as I sat alone at my desk.

As the years wore on, that day stood out as a pivotal point in my life. Suddenly everything changed. My place in the family was gone. I was like a bird over the ocean, eternally flying with no place to land. I played out the story over and over in my mind, trying to make sense of it. How could this have happened?

My foundation was shattered. The people I thought would always be there had slipped from my grasp. But as I and the few who remained sought to mend our hearts, I reached out for that one special hand. Jesus gently guided me away from the land of hurt and into a place he had chosen just for me.

## Encouragement

A great loss can spin our world out of control. Our anchor is gone and we're cast into space. Often we don't understand why. We just know the pain is overwhelming. Still, when we open our eyes and survey the wreckage, a familiar figure sits perched on the ruins, beckoning us near.

Jesus was no stranger to pain and loss. He suffered just as we do. But there's one loss he has promised will never happen: the loss of those who belong to him. He protects all the sheep in his fold. He binds up the wounds of those who are hurt. He heals all the bruises and gashes of life. The loving shepherd tends his flock.

## Your Story

Describe your most devastating loss.

What was the impact on your life?

How have you grown through this experience?

In what ways did God walk with you in the midst of your pain?

## Reflection

Even in the anguish of an overwhelming loss, God leads us
into a deeper life with him. This verse holds a comforting
promise. We will never slip from his hand, no matter what.
Reflect for a moment on the words of Jesus:

*This is the will of God,*
*that I should not lose even one of all those he has given me,*
*but that I should raise them up at the last day.*
*John 6:39 (NLT)*

How do you feel, knowing you will never be lost?


What other thoughts do you have about loss?


## A Special Prayer

Jesus—you see the heartache and pain in my life. Sometimes
it's almost unbearable, yet I know you will never leave me. Even
when I feel all alone, you are there. Please take me in your
arms, bandage my wounded soul, and give me your healing
rest. Keep me in your loving embrace forever. Amen.

# CHAPTER 22

# *Loving*

*A person standing alone
can be attacked and defeated,
but two can stand back-to-back and conquer.
Three are even better,
for a triple-braided cord is not easily broken.*
*Ecclesiastes 4:12 (NLT)*

Let's be honest. We just want to be loved. Society says we should be happy and fulfilled on our own, but something is missing. We yearn for the closeness that only another human can offer. How do we find it? Where is the love we crave?

We're willing to invest countless hours looking for someone with whom we can deeply connect. The search can be exhausting. Tears of loneliness sting our eyes as we beam a flashlight into the blackness of night, searching and coming up empty. And yet our quest continues.

## My Story

I was single and looking for companionship, but the man of my dreams was elusive. No matter where I looked, I couldn't find him. It was time for some serious prayer. "God, where is this mysterious man you have for me?"

At the same time, I was busy helping a local organization set up a new ministry. Part of my job was to scour the Internet for others with the same mission. And there he was—in California. He became one of my "research subjects." When the project ended, we kept in touch. One night he arose at 3:00 a.m. to declare his feelings in an e-mail titled "Sleepless in Fresno."

We realized we were called to the same ministry and to be partners in both life and work. Even before he moved to Colorado for our wedding, we set up our own non-profit organization. We knew God was uniting us for this purpose, and we couldn't imagine doing anything else.

## Encouragement

When God brings people together, there's a reason beyond companionship. Sure, he wants them to be happy and fulfilled together, yet his underlying purpose can be so much more. Perhaps he has a special project in mind for them. Maybe their example will inspire others. Whether it's starting a ministry or filling a specific need, God's hand is in it.

When we search for someone to love, why do we often consult God last? We look here and there, consult our friends, and test out the latest dating advice. But perhaps we are forgetting God's grand design. He calls us together for his purpose. A three-strand cord—two people and God—can accomplish great things and ultimately change the world. So why not include him from the beginning?

## Your Story

Think back on a special relationship. How did you become acquainted?

Were you looking on your own, or did you ask for God's help?

How did you sense God brought you together for a purpose?

What ultimately happened in that relationship?

## Reflection

God wants the best for us. He loves us and understands our desire for a special relationship. We can trust the outcome of his plans. Ponder the comfort of this verse:

*We know that in all things
God works for the good of those who love him,
who have been called according to his purpose.*
Romans 8:28 (NIV)

Looking back on your life and relationships, how has God worked everything together for your good?

What other thoughts do you have about loving and being loved?

## A Special Prayer

Jesus—I know you love me and are always with me. But you've also given me the desire to love and be loved by others. My heart longs for a close relationship with a special person. Guide me to one who is just right for me. Walk with us as we forge a strong bond together. Amen.

# CHAPTER 23

# *Stretching*

*I try to find common ground with everyone*
*doing everything I can to save some.*
*I do everything to spread the Good News*
*and share in its blessings.*
*1 Corinthians 9:22b-23 (NLT)*

Everybody's different. Just as no two snowflakes are the same, neither are any two people exactly alike. We have distinct ways of dressing, talking, and even worshipping God. That's part of the reason there are so many different Christian traditions and denominations.

We're comfortable with our own worship style. It fits us like a pair of old slippers. Perhaps it's all we've ever known. We may even think those "other" Christians are a little odd. Why would we want to step out and try something new? It could feel weird, we might look stupid, and the whole thing would just be embarrassing.

## My Story

I had definite opinions about church music. Organ music rising to the ceiling of a majestic cathedral was my idea of a spiritual experience. But my new husband loved to rock out with praise and worship bands. How could we solve this dilemma? Finally, we decided to look for two churches, one for him and one for me. We were determined to attend both every Sunday.

Anxiously, I stepped into the "other church" for the first time. The band was blaring, and everyone waved their hands over their heads, singing exuberantly. Little by little, I joined in. After a few months, I learned to move with the rhythm and clap a bit. But raising my arms in the air was just too much. Then one Sunday I gingerly lifted a hand in song. After that, it was easy.

Eventually, I was rewarded for my willingness to try something new. Learning different worship styles made my work easier. My husband and I spoke in many different churches, and now I could relate to everybody through our common experience.

## Encouragement

God doesn't let us stay in our comfort zones forever. He invites us to step out, move beyond our limits, and learn new skills. Then we can express our faith in fresh, unique, and innovative ways.

But he never leaves us to muddle through it alone. God has a vision for every single person, placing each of us in just the right spot so we can bloom. He lovingly prepares and guides us in each move we make, even as we stretch far beyond what we thought we could do.

## Your Story

When did you hesitate to step out and try something new?

What challenges did you bump against?

How did you make progress in your efforts?

Where did you see God in the midst of your struggles?

## Reflection

It's never easy to try something different. The older we get, the harder it is. But staying in a rut isn't what God has in mind for us. He asks us to move with him through life's adventures. Quietly give prayerful thought to this verse:

*"I know all the things you do.*
*I have seen your love, your faith,*
*your service, and your patient endurance.*
*And I can see your constant improvement in all these things."*
*Revelation 2:19 (NLT)*

How is your life different today because you stepped out and accepted God's invitation to grow?

What other thoughts do you have about stretching in your faith?

## A Special Prayer

Jesus—I know you want me to try new things. From my perspective, though, that's a little scary! Could we walk together, just a small step at a time? Lead me in fresh directions and help me experience new horizons. If you'll stay with me, I know I can do it. Amen.

# CHAPTER 24

# *Serving*

*Work willingly at whatever you do,
as though you were working for the Lord
rather than for people.*
*Colossians 3:23 (NLT)*

"What's in it for me?"

That's the time-honored slogan of the American consumer. Sometimes we're so busy looking out for ourselves, we walk right past opportunities to serve. In our quest to get more, we forget to give. Even at church, we're often more concerned about being fed spiritually than helping others.

Perhaps we hesitate because generosity has a cost. Maybe we're not sure we can bear the sacrifice of service. Yet if we stop and think about the sacrifice Jesus made, our inconvenience and concern for ourselves suddenly seem trivial. Is a "taker" mentality really appropriate when we worship the one who gave the ultimate gift?

᧬   ᧬   ᧬   ᧬   ᧬   ᧬   ᧬

## My Story

My husband was edgy. He had been out of sorts all day on our get-away. As we walked along a secluded path, he finally blurted out, "I think God is calling us to full-time ministry. But how could we afford it?" I thought for a minute and assured him, "There's a way."

And there was. Scaling down financially became a great adventure. We parked the cell phone in the glove compartment, buying minutes once a year. The cable TV gave way to free movies from the library, and restaurant coupons were newfound treasures. We became a one-car family, creatively managing our schedules so no one was left without wheels.

Our new life of service was definitely worth the cost. As we worked together, I privately thought of myself as a communion server, symbolically offering the body and blood of Christ to those I knew or happened to meet. I wasn't obvious about it, and they probably never knew what I was doing. Yet this hidden service brought me much joy.

## Encouragement

It doesn't really matter what's in it for us. The real question is, what's in it for God and those who need him? Sometimes the results of our service aren't visible, yet he sees them. A life that honors God is one that gives more than it takes. It is one that makes cheerful, willing sacrifices in order to serve him and others.

Teresa of Avila, a famous Christian from centuries ago, said the only hands and feet Christ has on earth are ours. What a lovely thought. Our service to others is such a powerful way for God to show his love and care in the world. So let's flex those muscles and get moving!

## Your Story

What have been your most significant areas of service?

How have you struggled with giving instead of getting?

What have you given up to serve God more fully?

When have you sensed God calling you to serve him even more?

## Reflection

Even when we serve others in humility and quietness, God sees and appreciates our efforts. He recognizes and rejoices over a giving spirit. Consider what this verse says to you:

*God is not unjust;*
*he will not forget your work*
*and the love you have shown him*
*as you have helped his people*
*and continue to help them.*
*Hebrews 6:10 (NIV)*

In what ways do you think God delights over your service to others?

What other thoughts do you have about serving?

## A Special Prayer

Jesus—my hands and feet are ready to serve you. Put me to work! There is so much pain in the world. Surely I can help soothe at least a little of it. Guide me in the direction I could do the most good. And most of all, be there with me. Amen.

# CHAPTER 25

# *Voicing*

*"I am the voice of one calling in the wilderness,
'Make straight the way for the Lord.'"*
*John 1:23b (NIV)*

"Here's the microphone. Tell us what you think!"

For the average person, speaking in public is so distasteful, it ranks right up there with paying taxes and dying. Yet for many of us, even expressing ourselves in private can be a challenge. Do we have anything important to say? Will anyone care?

For some, speaking our minds comes naturally. We know what to say and how to say it. For others, it's not so simple. We may be reluctant to talk because of negative past experiences. Or maybe we don't know what to say, or we believe our voice is of no consequence. Regardless of the reason, something is lost in the silence.

## My Story

As a child, I struggled with having a voice. In my family, personal expression was not only discouraged, but sometimes even punished. I came to believe I didn't have anything worthwhile to say. Even during my political career, it was difficult to speak up. Others voiced their thoughts easily, but even sharing a simple opinion without my written notes seemed impossible.

As I moved into ministry with my husband, the struggle continued. I felt overshadowed by his talents and had trouble coming up with ideas of my own. Gradually, he became the focus of our ministry and I felt lost. A sabbatical retreat helped me find my voice and the confidence to speak what God gave me to say.

Yet in the greater ministry world, my voice still felt muted because I was a woman. Initially, I tried to become "one of the boys." That didn't solve the problem. Then an advisor said, "Look at the holy women in history, even Mother Teresa. Because God was with them, they were unstoppable."

I felt encouraged.

## Encouragement

How can we overcome our reluctance to speak up and let our voices sing? Perhaps we hesitate because we discount our value to God and the world. But he has uniquely created each person with a message to share. Maybe it's time to remove the demeaning "70% off" sale stickers we've plastered to our foreheads and tell the stories we are meant to tell.

Having the courage to speak requires faith and trust. Perhaps this is one of the great secrets of devout men and women through the centuries. Their voices rose from deep within, speaking what God had given them to say. Some were well received. Some were not. Yet all were grounded in a deep faith that simply knew and loved God—no more, no less.

## Your Story

Can you describe a time you struggled to reveal your true voice?

What do you think was the cause of this difficulty?

What strides have you made in expressing truth?

How has God helped you release your voice?

## Reflection

Finding our voices and learning to sing can feel daunting. Often it's easier to do just about anything than speak up. Yet nothing is impossible for a soul abandoned to God. Spend a few moments with this passage:

> *"Don't be afraid! Speak out! Don't be silent!*
> *For I am with you,*
> *and no one will attack and harm you…"*
> *Acts 18:9b-10a (NLT)*

How does your sense of safety in God's arms give you the courage to speak?

What other thoughts do you have about expressing your voice?

## A Special Prayer

Jesus—my soul cries out to you as I struggle to express my true voice. Help me to hold nothing back as you teach me to sing. Draw open the curtains of my life and let me bravely speak the words you have given me. Hold my hand as I courageously walk onto the stage of life. Amen.

# CHAPTER 26

# Persevering

*Patient endurance is what you need now,*
*so that you will continue to do God's will.*
*Then you will receive all that he has promised.*
*Hebrews 10:36 (NLT)*

Do you ever feel like giving up? Do you wonder if anyone cares about the work you do? Sometimes it's hard to get up every morning and slog through the day for a job that doesn't seem to matter to anyone.

God has a purpose for each of us. Usually it involves service—paid or otherwise. Although the work may sound fun and exciting, detours and snags can put a dent in our enthusiasm. Where is the serenity and contentment we expected from serving him?

## My Story

Starting a ministry with my husband was the hardest thing I ever did. Being accustomed to quick success, I didn't plan on struggling year after year just to get the basics in place. Sometimes my frustration overflowed. I wanted my life to matter, but at this rate, how would that ever happen?

From the beginning, our ministry was a challenging venture. The message of Christlikeness was a tough sell. For many believers, wanting to be like Jesus didn't even make the radar screen. Marketing an intimate relationship with God was definitely an uphill battle.

But deep inside I knew this was our calling. I couldn't imagine doing anything else. A different job simply wasn't an option. That conviction kept me going, day after day, even when my work didn't seem to make any difference at all.

## Encouragement

God doesn't promise to fulfill our dreams of unlimited success. We may never see the final outcome of our work. And yet it is impossible to calculate the depth, breadth, and significance of a life devoted to Christ. In the midst of our struggles, he offers us peace, joy, and his own presence in our journey.

Thus, we persevere. God has given each of us a race to run, and we must put aside everything that gets in the way. When we reach the finish line, Jesus will be there saying, "Well done, good and faithful servant."

## Your Story

Describe your most significant challenge.

Where were your greatest frustrations?

How did you persevere through these obstacles?

What long-term impact do you think God saw in your work?

## Reflection

Persevering is never easy. Tackling substantial difficulties is no picnic. Still, if our heart's desire is to grow spiritually, it's part of the job description. Reflect prayerfully on this passage:

*Consider it pure joy, my brothers and sisters,*
*whenever you face trials of many kinds,*
*because you know that*
*the testing of your faith produces perseverance.*
*Let perseverance finish its work*
*so that you may be mature and complete,*
*not lacking anything.*
*James 1:2-4 (NIV)*

In what ways have tough challenges shaped your spiritual life and brought you closer to God?

What other thoughts do you have about persevering?

## A Special Prayer

Jesus—I'm overwhelmed by so many obstacles! Each day brings new races for me to run. Yet I am not alone. You are here, encouraging and cheering me on. Your love keeps me on track. Help me to persevere, to keep on until I have finished the race. Amen.

# CHAPTER 27

# *Resting*

*Those who live in the shelter of the Most High*
*will find rest in the shadow of the Almighty.*
*This I declare about the LORD:*
*He alone is my refuge, my place of safety;*
*he is my God, and I trust him.*
*Psalm 91:1-2 (NLT)*

Can we ever understand the trials of life? We can fuss and fight. We can analyze and probe. In the end, though, some things are simply beyond our explanation. Only God sees and fully comprehends the mysteries of our lives.

If we're honest, we'll admit that sometimes life is just tough. And it doesn't get any easier with age. Often the losses feel like more than we can bear. Whether relationships, finances, health, or a myriad of other problems, our hardships seem unexplainable. How could this happen? Shouldn't life be easier?

## My Story

Of all the difficulties in my life, I struggled most with losing part of my family. There were reasons the relationships were damaged, but no matter how I analyzed it, my heart was broken. Slowly I realized God had allowed this to happen. He had a reason. I just didn't know what it was yet.

God reminded me of another hurtful situation in the far distant past. After many years, I finally understood his purpose in that circumstance and knew it had turned out for the best. Someday, I realized, my current heartache would be the same.

Eventually I found peace. The words of William Wordsworth comforted me: "Though nothing can bring back the hour of splendor in the grass, of glory in the flower, we will grieve not; rather find strength in what remains behind."

The past could not be recaptured, and the future was a tapestry yet to be woven. My soul rested in God's hands.

## Encouragement

Who can see into the heart of God? No one can understand why hurtful things happen. But we can have peace. After a long, hard journey, after much prayer and soul-searching, we can come to the realization that God is all we really have. Nothing more. Nothing less.

When difficulties arise, as they surely will, we can echo the words of Job: "The Lord gives, and the Lord takes away. Blessed be the name of the Lord." (Job 1:21 par) The peace that passes all understanding can finally be ours when we rest in his arms, knowing that whatever happens, however much it hurts, God's will is perfect.

## Your Story

What has been the greatest struggle you've faced?

How have you tried to explain it to yourself?

Describe the journey you walked to resolve it.

What have you learned about God in the process?

## Reflection

Let's face it—we can't really control anything. Our only stability is a deep and abiding trust in God. Open the depths of your heart to this passage:

> *Truly my soul finds rest in God;*
> *my salvation comes from him.*
> *Truly he is my rock and my salvation;*
> *he is my fortress, I will never be shaken.*
> *Psalm 62:1-2 (NIV)*

How can you discover a rest so profound that life's trials can't shake you?

What other thoughts do you have about resting?

## A Special Prayer

Jesus—you are my rock and my salvation. I rest only in you. As I move through the deep waters of life, be with me. Sustain and comfort me as you give me your unique special peace. May I always rest in you, knowing you are my God and will be with me forever. Amen.

# CHAPTER 28

# *Emerging*

*Those who know your name trust in you,*
*for you, O LORD, do not abandon*
*those who search for you.*
*Psalm 9:10 (NLT)*

Wherever we look these days, we find a hunger for anything even remotely spiritual. The latest books seem to fly off the shelves. Seminars boast record attendance. Whether or not we admit it, we feel a deep longing to be connected to something greater than ourselves. As we search for that spiritual connection, our God-given individuality begins to emerge and mold the shape of something sacred.

Each of us has a unique spiritual story. Perhaps we have always known God's love, and our lives have followed a steady course to an ever deeper relationship with him. Or maybe we've passed through difficult or tragic circumstances and discovered Jesus as our companion along the journey. Either way, each event in our story is unmistakably our own.

Up to this point, your memory and imagination have been sparked by similarities to the events in my life. But each of us travels a different path. Your story has twists and turns that are deeply personal and uniquely shaped to your spiritual life.

It's time for your one-of-a-kind story to emerge. This chapter offers two sets of general questions. Use them to gather your thoughts and ponder circumstances that are distinctly yours. If you have more experiences you'd like to consider, feel free to explore them too.

## Your Special Story

How would you describe an important event or time in your life?

What were the enjoyable or challenging aspects?

In what ways did it shape your spiritual life?

How did you sense God's presence in your situation?

## Another Special Story

What was another important event or time in your life?

What were the especially pleasant or difficult aspects?

How was your spiritual life influenced?

Where did you find God in this circumstance?

## Reflection

When we grow spiritually, we begin to emerge as the unique individuals we were created to be. Both joys and hardships appear along the way. But if we look carefully, we see Jesus by our side. Ponder this verse for a moment in silence.

*"Be still, and know that I am God…"*
*Psalm 46:10 (NIV)*

Deep in your soul, how do you know God is who he says he is?

What other thoughts do you have about your special stories?

## A Special Prayer

Jesus—I've searched for you like a precious treasure. I've looked for you in every corner of my life. And you have honored that quest, even as you sheltered and protected me like an emerging butterfly. Keep me on your special path as you draw ever nearer to me in love. Amen.

# CHAPTER 29

# Looking Back

*"I am the light of the world. If you follow me,
you won't have to walk in darkness,
because you will have the light that leads to life."*
*John 8:12 (NLT)*

Okay—let's be honest. Who among us hasn't stumbled alone in the dark at some time in our lives? Wandering in the shadows is a common experience. But here's the good news: whether we simply reach out to flip the light switch or meander slowly toward the dawn, our path moves ever closer to God.

When we're caught up in a swirl of trouble and doubt, it's hard to see what God is doing. Could it be that he likes to work undercover? Or maybe he enjoys surprising us when we least expect it? Whatever his method or motive, God's hand eventually becomes visible in the experiences and events that shape our lives.

## Christ Quest Time Map

Now, let's put all the pieces together by mapping out a timeline of your personal spiritual journey. Here are a few tips to get you started:

Go back through the chapters of this book. Make note of the important events, milestones, and other significant moments in your life.

On a blank paper, draw a winding line to mark the path of your journey. Fill in your Christ Quest experiences as milestones on the line.

Consider marking your story with symbols. Here are a few possibilities:

- An exclamation point for an important event or achievement
- A single arrow for a breakthrough or significant insight
- A cross for a "God moment" or spiritual encounter
- A two-sided arrow for a time of uncertainty or struggle

Place these symbols, or any others you choose, on your journey line to mark the major moments of your story. Briefly describe each experience, memory, and event. Listen for God's voice as you honor each milestone.

Then look over your map for patterns, themes, and insights. Write down whatever you see, think, or feel about the tapestry of your life. When you're finished, sit in silence for a few moments and invite God to reveal his presence in your Christ Quest journey.

## Your Christ Quest Time Map

## Observations about Your Journey

## Reflection

Hidden truths emerge when we map out the timeline of our lives. God has given us great joy and has also led us through deep pain. As we watch his hand weaving together the threads of our lives, we begin to glimpse a divine purpose. Consider these words of Jesus:

> *I am the true grapevine, and my Father is the gardener.*
> *He cuts off every branch of mine that doesn't produce fruit,*
> *and he prunes the branches that do bear fruit*
> *so they will produce even more.*
> *John 15:1-2 (NLT)*

Looking back over your journey, where has God pruned you?

How have you grown as a result?

What other thoughts do you have about your journey?

## A Special Prayer

Jesus—we've traveled so far together! I see you at work in my life from the beginning, even before I was born. You are indeed my proud parent. Thank you for caring for me, for bringing me through deep waters to rest in your healing light. Keep your loving hand on me as we finish our trek together. Amen.

CHAPTER 30

# Moving Forward

*"This is my command—*
*Be strong and courageous!*
*Do not be afraid or discouraged.*
*For the LORD your God*
*is with you wherever you go."*
*Joshua 1:9 (NLT)*

God isn't finished with us yet. Not even close! He has brought us this far, and there is still a long way to go. We may think our days haven't counted for much up to this point. Perhaps we've seen more than our fair share of heartache and despair. Or maybe we feel positive and optimistic about our lives. Either way, it's time to move forward. We can look ahead with anticipation to see where God will lead us next.

Jesus himself lived in relative obscurity for 30 years before God called him to public ministry. If not for the events surrounding his birth, who would have guessed he would become the Savior of the world? And so it is with us. It's never too late to discover God's purpose for our lives and to walk the path he has prepared for each of us.

## Your Journey Forward

As you consider your next steps, you have important questions to answer and issues to address. Spend a few minutes prayerfully considering your life. Think back over your spiritual journey timeline. Consider where you are today. Finally, reflect on the plans you believe God has for you. Here are some questions to help you get started.

## Where Have You Been?

What has been the best experience of your life journey so far?

Which event has proven to be the most difficult?

Where were the pivotal points in your timeline?

## Where Are You Now?

In what ways is your past influencing your present?

What spiritual themes are reflected in your story, and in who you are now?

Where do you see God's hand in your life today?

## Where Are You Going?

How has God prepared you for the future through the experiences of your spiritual journey?

What personal difficulties and issues need to be addressed so you can move forward?

What steps will you take to grow into the person God calls you to be?

## Reflection

You have come a long way in your quest for Christ. There have been good times and bad. In the end, you can rest in the arms of Jesus, knowing you have run the race of faith with a sincere heart. You are in good company. Even though the Apostle Paul struggled throughout his life, in the end he was able to say:

> *I have fought the good fight,*
> *I have finished the race,*
> *I have kept the faith.*
> *2 Timothy 4:7 (NIV)*

As you complete the rest of your race, what are your spiritual hopes and dreams?

What other thoughts do you have about moving forward?

## A Special Prayer

Jesus—thank you for bringing me to this day. Through my journey I've tried to walk forward with confidence, only to be stranded in valleys of pain. Yet through it all you have been with me. You have guided me, protected me, comforted me, and set me back on my feet again. Let us walk hand in hand, together into eternity. Amen.

# Closing Thoughts

Wow—you've made it all the way through the book! It's been quite a journey, reviewing the spiritual peaks and valleys of your life. You've marked milestone achievements and recalled countless smiles and tears. Each step offered a fresh glimpse of the path ahead. God has led you on a journey to himself—a journey that isn't over yet.

As we watch our lives unfold over the coming months and years, let's remember these words written by Augustine of Hippo, a Christian who lived more than 1600 years ago:

*God, you have made us for yourself,*
*and our hearts are restless*
*till they find their rest in you.*

Augustine believed there is a God-shaped hole in every person, and we won't be happy until it's filled. In sharing our stories and struggles together, we've come to embrace this truth.

As we continue along our individual paths, let's reflect for a minute on this reassuring word from the Apostle Paul. It's one of the verses the mayor told me to look up years ago, at the dawn of my walk with Christ. Perhaps you will find it comforting too.

> *Do not be anxious about anything, but in every situation,*
> *by prayer and petition, with thanksgiving,*
> *present your requests to God.*
> *And the peace of God, which transcends all understanding,*
> *will guard your hearts and your minds in Christ Jesus.*
> *Philippians 4:6-7 (NIV)*

Now, continue your quest for Christ. You will walk through delight and distress, triumph and thorns. At the end of your journey, Jesus will be there, waiting to welcome you home.

Go in peace.

# Four Session Lesson Plan

The spiritual life is full of twists and turns, joys and challenges. As you strive to uncover the deeper insights of the Christian journey, consider using this small group study at your church or other ministry setting.

*On a Quest for Christ* can help participants recall pivotal points in their lives that have shaped who they are today. They'll be able to see when Christ met them along the way and how he can be trusted to guide them into the future. The discussion questions could be especially useful to help a newly formed group get to know one another and bond quickly. Souls will be refreshed as the group is led to places of healing and hope.

This lesson plan covers twenty selected chapters, including the Christ Quest Time Map. Detailed notes are provided and a Leader's Guide is included at the end. Feel free to use this study plan or adapt it to meet your group's needs.

## Session One
## Encountering God

Today's session is about recalling how and when we committed ourselves to Christ, which can happen at any time in our lives. Perhaps we remember our personal conversion stories, back when we were new believers. Or if we have followed Christ since childhood, we may think of a time of renewed or increased commitment.

Our first meeting is a good occasion to remember this important time in our lives. Maybe we'll even notice some similar experiences. We will cover six chapters from our book, organized into three discussions. I'll introduce each one and read a few selections. Then let's talk!

### Part 1: Turning and Searching (Chapters 8 and 9)

Before we begin, I'd like to read this scripture passage:

> *"Ask and it will be given to you;*
> *seek and you will find;*
> *knock and the door will be opened to you.*
> *For everyone who asks receives;*
> *the one who seeks finds;*
> *and to the one who knocks,*
> *the door will be opened.*
> *Matthew 7:7-8 (NIV)*

Some of us were raised in the faith from an early age. Some were not. For some, a time comes when we suddenly believe. Others simply begin to take the faith more seriously. In either case, we often start to search for answers when difficult situations appear in our lives.

I'll read Lisa's stories about Turning and Searching. *(Leader: please read "My Story" from chapters 8 and 9, then discuss the following questions.)*

Did you ever experience a crisis that caused you to re-evaluate your life? What happened?

What were you searching for, and where did you look for it?

### Part 2: Encountering and Exploring (Chapters 10 and 11)

Here's another scripture verse as we consider these two chapters:

> *If you search for [God] with*
> *all your heart and soul,*
> *you will find him.*
> *Deuteronomy 4:29b (NLT)*

Some of us have dramatic conversion experiences. This often occurs if we are older when we make a decision for Christ. Or perhaps we have always considered ourselves Christian but one day arrived at a point of deeper commitment. Regardless of how it happens, this is a pivotal point in our spiritual journeys.

Now I'll share Lisa's stories about Encountering and Exploring. *(Leader: please read "My Story" from chapters 10 and 11, then discuss the following questions.)*

Did you have a conversion experience or was there a specific time when you committed more fully to Christ? What did that time in your life look like?

How did you sense God leading you into a deeper relationship with him?

### Part 3: Pursuing and Learning (Chapters 12 and 15)

As we prepare for our third discussion, let's ponder this scripture verse:

*Whatever you have learned or received or heard from me,*
*or seen in me—put it into practice.*
*And the God of peace will be with you.*
*Philippians 4:9 (NIV)*

After becoming committed to Christ, we all have one trait in common: we're thirsty to learn more. So, we seek out lots of ways to get to know him better. Often other believers come alongside us to help.

Here are Lisa's stories about Pursuing and Learning. *(Leader: please read "My Story" from chapters 12 and 15, then discuss the following questions.)*

What opportunities did God put in your path to help you learn about him?

Have you had a spiritual guide or special group of friends that made a difference in your life? How did they help you?

### Conclusion: Other Experiences of Encountering God

These three chapters from the book described Lisa's journey of making a personal commitment to follow Christ. Does anyone have a similar experience of encountering God that they haven't shared yet?

Thanks so much for being here today. Be sure to write down your experiences about encountering God in your journal. You'll want to remember them when we fill in our time maps in a later session.

## Session Two
## Struggling with God

Today we're talking about issues that cause us to struggle with God and in our faith. The topics we will cover are not necessarily related to each other. But these are all difficulties that can keep us from getting to know God and cloud our ongoing relationship with him.

The chapters in this session are all struggles from Lisa's faith journey. Yours may be very different. We'll be sure to talk about those too. As before, we're covering six chapters from the book in this session. They are organized into three discussions. After I open each one with a couple of selections, feel free to chime in!

### Part 1: Birthing and Earning (Chapters 1 and 4)

As we start our first discussion, let's ponder this scripture passage:

*"Give careful thought to your ways.*
*You have planted much, but have harvested little.*
*You eat, but never have enough.*
*You drink, but never have your fill.*
*You put on clothes, but are not warm.*
*You earn wages, only to put them in a purse with holes in it."*
*Haggai 1:5b-6 (NIV)*

Your birth circumstances are important to your spiritual journey story. Some are born into warm, loving homes. Some are not. Some are born into Christian families. Some are not. Our early beginnings can shape how we see the world and our future spiritual life.

Also, many of us try to earn our way to happiness. As Americans, it's quite common to value our definition of success above all else. But where is God in all this focus on achievement?

Let me read Lisa's stories about Birthing and Earning. (*Leader: please read "My Story" from chapters 1 and 4, then discuss the following questions.*)

What kinds of challenges did you face with your family of origin?

What are some things you have tried to earn? Were you looking for wealth, success, love or something else?

## Part 2: Ignoring and Judging (Chapters 2 and 6)

Let's think about this scripture passage while listening to the next two chapters:

> *Such is the destiny of all who forget God;*
> *so perishes the hope of the godless.*
> *What they trust in is fragile;*
> *what they rely on is a spider's web.*
> *They lean on the web, but it gives way;*
> *they cling to it, but it does not hold.*
> *Job 8:13-15 (NIV)*

Here we'll talk about a couple more situations that can distract us from God. It's not uncommon for people to ignore God or run away from him altogether. Some believers walk with God when they are young, but then fall away for a time.

Also, judging others is a common activity and easy to do. But beware—our judgments about other people can blind us to our own spiritual struggles.

Let's check out Lisa's stories about Ignoring and Judging. *(Leader: please read "My Story" from chapters 2 and 6, then discuss the following questions.)*

Have you ever doubted God or walked away from him? What happened?

Has your faith life ever been affected by your own judgmental attitude? How did that hinder your relationship with God and others around you?

### Part 3: Belonging and Voicing (Chapters 5 and 25)

As we head into our third discussion, let's think about this scripture verse:

> *For none of us lives for ourselves alone,*
> *and none of us dies for ourselves alone.*
> *If we live, we live for the Lord;*
> *and if we die, we die for the Lord.*
> *So, whether we live or die, we belong to the Lord.*
> *Romans 14:7-8 (NIV)*

Here are two more situations that sometimes cause us to struggle with God. Many of us have a strong need to fit in. We just want to belong somewhere. But that desire for acceptance by a group can take precedence over our relationship with God.

Also, the struggle to be heard, understood, and valued can be an issue. Often it takes years to develop a unique voice and discover how our gifts can best serve God. It's not easy to remember that God always hears, understands, and cherishes us, regardless of our contributions to the world.

Here are Lisa's stories about Belonging and Voicing. *(Leader: please read "My Story" from chapters 5 and 25, then discuss the following questions.)*

Did you ever feel like you just didn't belong? How did that affect you?

Can you describe a time when you struggled to find your true voice? How did God remind you of his constant love while you waited for answers?

## Conclusion: Other Experiences of Struggling with God

Our discussions today describe six different examples of struggling with God. Does anyone have an experience of struggling with God that they haven't shared yet?

Thanks for being here with us. Don't forget to write down your experiences about struggling with God in your journal. We'll be doing our time maps soon, so you'll want to be able to include these important areas of your life.

## Session Three
## Walking with God

Today's session is about growing into a mature faith. As we journey with God, we encounter many circumstances that help us to grow. Our troubles may be incredibly difficult at times but they are necessary to help us strengthen our faith.

As we consider this, let's talk about a few issues from Lisa's personal walk with God. I know your stories will be different. We'll be sure to touch on these during the discussion time.

We're going to cover six more chapters from the book, two at a time with three discussion opportunities in between. You're invited to join in the conversation after I open each one.

### Part 1: Obeying and Stretching (Chapters 19 and 23)

Let's consider this scripture passage as we begin our study:

> *Live a life worthy of the Lord and please him in every way:*
> *bearing fruit in every good work,*
> *growing in the knowledge of God,*
> *being strengthened with all power*
> *according to his glorious might.*
> *Colossians 1:10-11a (NIV)*

As our faith deepens, God may ask us to obey his wishes in ways we may not understand. It takes courage to forge ahead into the unknown. God may even ask us to do new things we'd rather not try. But we can't grow unless we stretch, and stretching helps to prepare us for what lies ahead.

Let's read Lisa's stories about Obeying and Stretching. *(Leader: please read "My Story" from chapters 19 and 23, then discuss the following questions.)*

Has God ever asked you to do something totally unexpected, and you didn't know why? Did you ever find out his purpose in asking you?

What challenges have you faced in stepping out and trying something new?

## Part 2: Forsaking and Standing (Chapters 17 and 18)

Here is a scripture verse for us to keep in mind during this next section:

> *"Never will I leave you; never will I forsake you."*
> *So we say with confidence,*
> *"The Lord is my helper; I will not be afraid."*
> *Hebrews 13:5b-6a (NIV)*

Sometimes, as we move deeper with Christ, we're called to give some things up. Perhaps it's our independence, relationships, or maybe material things. There will also be times, as we step ahead in faith, when we have to take a stand. It could be on a public issue or with a friend or co-worker.

Here are Lisa's stories about Forsaking and Standing. *(Leader: please read "My Story" from chapters 17 and 18, then discuss the following questions.)*

As your relationship with God has grown, what were some areas of your life he has asked you to forsake?

Have you ever had to take a difficult stand? What emotional and spiritual struggles did you endure?

## Part 3: Healing and Resting (Chapters 14 and 27)

I'd like us to dwell on this last scripture passage:

*Truly my soul finds rest in God; my salvation comes from him.*
*Truly he is my rock and my salvation; he is my fortress,*
*I will never be shaken.*
*Psalm 62:1-2 (NIV)*

As we move through the various challenges of our Christian lives, we may notice that a feeling of peace begins to grow. We feel steadier in our faith—more mature. Even the most difficult experiences can lead to personal healing, acceptance, and deeper spiritual growth.

Let me share Lisa's stories from Healing and Resting. *(Leader: please read "My Story" from chapters 14 and 27, then discuss the following questions.)*

Describe how you've worked through a painful experience to find healing in God.

Is it really possible to discover a rest so profound that life's trials can't shake it? How?

## Conclusion: Other Experiences of Walking with God

These three segments from the book described part of Lisa's journey to a more mature faith. Does anyone have a story of walking with God that they haven't shared yet?

I've really appreciated everyone's participation in this class. Before our next meeting, write down your experiences about walking with God. Be sure to bring your journal with you to the next session so we can draw our time maps.

## Session Four
## Looking Back and Moving Forward

Today we're going to wrap up our four-session series by drawing our Christ Quest Time Maps. Each person's map will be a reflection of his or her own personal spiritual journey. After we take a few minutes to share our completed maps, we'll chat about what may be happening next in our lives.

First, let's have a quick review for those who may have missed some of our meetings and also to help jog our memories.

### Part 1: Quick Review

In our sessions, we've talked about three main spiritual themes:

- Our decisions to follow Christ
- Our spiritual struggles
- Our deepening walk with God

In the past few sessions, we've discussed the events that caused us to seek Christ, how we searched for him, and ways we got to know him better.

We've talked about our struggles with God. These occurred with our families of origin, trying to earn love, ignoring God, judging others, wanting to belong, and seeking our voices.

We also considered ways that we've matured in our walk with God. We discussed obeying his requests, stretching and growing, forsaking things that mattered to us, taking difficult stands, personal healing, and resting in God.

These specific examples were from the book. We also shared many other amazing personal stories together, thanks to everyone's great participation and transparency.

### Part 2: Our Christ Quest Time Maps

Now it's time to put it all together. We're going to take a few minutes to draw our Christ Quest Time Maps. Before we get started, let's consider these two scripture verses:

*"I am the light of the world.*
*If you follow me, you won't have to walk in darkness,*
*because you will have the light that leads to life."*
*John 8:12 (NLT)*

*I am the true grapevine,*
*and my Father is the gardener.*
*He cuts off every branch of mine*
*that doesn't produce fruit,*
*and he prunes the branches that do bear fruit*
*so they will produce even more.*
*John 15:1-2 (NLT)*

Before you draw your map, think back on the topics we've talked about. Be sure to look at your journal notes from our previous sessions. Then, on a new page, draw a winding line to mark the path of your journey. Mark your Christ Quest experiences as milestones on the line.

You can also use symbols on your journey line to mark the major moments of your story. Here are some for you to consider:

- An exclamation point for an important event or achievement
- A single arrow for a breakthrough or significant insight
- A cross for a "God moment" or spiritual encounter
- A two-sided arrow for a time of uncertainty or struggle

Briefly describe each experience, memory, and event. Be sure to listen for God's voice as you honor each milestone. When you're done, look over your map for patterns, themes, and insights. *(Leader: it may help the group if you draw out a simple map ahead of time to show them how the process works.)*

### Part 3: Looking Back and Moving Forward

Now we'll talk about our maps and where we're going from here. Let's spend a few minutes reflecting together on these questions. After you go home, you can meditate on them some more.

### Where Have You Been?

What has been the best experience of your life journey so far?

Which event has proven to be the most difficult?

Where were the pivotal points in your timeline?

### Where Are You Now?

In what ways is your past influencing your present?

What spiritual themes are reflected in your story, and in who you are now?

Where do you see God's hand in your life today?

## Where Are You Going?

How has God prepared you for the future through the experiences of your spiritual journey?

What personal difficulties and issues need to be addressed so you can move forward?

What steps will you take to grow into the person God calls you to be?

I'd like to thank everyone for taking this journey. I hope our time together has helped you see how God has sustained you and given you new hope for what may lie ahead.

As we depart, I'd like to leave you with two final scripture verses. First, in the words of Joshua:

> *"This is my command—be strong and courageous!*
> *Do not be afraid or discouraged.*
> *For the LORD your God is with you wherever you go."*
> *Joshua 1:9 (NLT)*

Lastly, in the words of the Apostle Paul:

> *I have fought the good fight,*
> *I have finished the race,*
> *I have kept the faith.*
> *2 Timothy 4:7 (NIV)*

May God bless each of you as you continue on your own special journey.

## Leader's Guide

Thank you for leading a study group using *On a Quest for Christ: Tracing the Footsteps of Your Spiritual Journey*. Here are a few tips and suggestions to help you get organized.

The lesson plan envisions a one-hour class. In the first three sessions each segment is around ten minutes with extra time for opening and closing comments. The fourth session may require more flexibility. Generally, fifteen minutes should be enough for the map, followed by discussions in ten-minute increments. If you prefer longer sessions, you may cover additional chapters or increase the discussion time.

The lesson plan also contains a suggested opening, explaining how the class is structured and what will be covered. You are welcome to modify it as needed for your group. If newcomers attend a later class, you may want to review the opening to get them up to speed.

Prayers may be included at the beginning, end, or both. Feel free to lead the prayer time as best fits your group.

Each session includes six chapters. I've found that it works well for the discussion leader to read aloud the "My Story" segments from each chapter, presenting two at a time. Hearing stories can help the participants to recall their own experiences and encourages them to share.

Although you may provide writing paper with pens and pencils, it's easier to ask each participant to bring a journal to all sessions. It is important that group members write down their responses to the discussion questions, along with other observations they have. These notes will be used in the last session to construct each individual's Christ Quest Time Map.

Be sure to establish a safe environment for sharing. Participants may be talking about sensitive areas of their lives. So, don't forget to address this during the first session and remind the group at later meetings. If the participants don't already know one another well, consider sharing a meal prior to each meeting. Eating together can often help people feel more comfortable and relaxed.

Finally, I've included a session opening for you to consider. Feel free to modify it to fit your particular group:

Welcome to our study. I'm looking forward to our four sessions together as we look at our personal faith journeys.

Our class is based on the book, *On a Quest for Christ: Tracing the Footsteps of Your Spiritual Journey* by Lisa Aré Wulf. You aren't required to buy it but that might be helpful since we're not doing all of the chapters during our time together. If you'd like to have a book, you can purchase one through Amazon or other retailers. We will also have copies available here.

In this class, we will condense this 30-day devotional guide down to four sessions. In each session we'll do several selected chapters. As we work together, we'll identify major spiritual events, issues and turning points in our lives.

The book is organized chronologically around the author's own spiritual story. Many chapters may resonate with you, but your personal story is unique.

Our discussions will be starting points for you to consider how the lessons relate to your own life.

Most chapters include a short story from the author's journey. I'll read them two at a time as we consider different aspects of the spiritual life. Then feel free to chime in about your own experience with the topic.

Our first session is called "Encountering God." We'll explore either our conversion stories or the circumstances that prompted us to make a serious commitment to our faith.

In the second session, we'll talk about "Struggling with God." During this time, we'll identify distractions and challenges we've faced in our Christian lives.

Our third topic is "Walking with God" and ways our faith has matured over the years. We'll discuss challenges we've overcome and whether we feel more settled in our faith today than we did as new believers.

During our fourth session, we'll put everything together as we think back on our lives—where we started, our challenges, and our growth. Then we'll draw our "Christ Quest Time Maps" that will pinpoint the significant events of our Christian journeys. Finally, we'll look at where each of us seems to be headed spiritually.

Be sure to bring a journal or other writing materials with you to each meeting to record important moments and events in your spiritual life. You will want to have these notes available as you draw your own personal time map in our last session.

Lastly, remember that confidentiality is important. We'll be discussing some personal and sensitive experiences. So, we need to maintain a safe and respectful environment. You don't need to talk if you don't want to. But be sure to honor each other's confidentiality. Remember—what is heard here stays here!

Any questions before we get started?

Thanks again for considering this study. You're welcome to contact me at lisa@LisaAreWulf.com with any thoughts, questions or ideas. I'd love to hear from you! God be with you as you lead others on this amazing journey, the quest for Christ.

# About the Author

A uniquely creative and transparent speaker, Lisa Aré Wulf has shared her journey with Christian women's groups throughout the country. She and her husband, Calvin, have spoken in churches across the denominational spectrum and their articles appeared in dozens of publications.

Before entering the ministry, Lisa was elected twice to the Colorado Springs City Council. She is also a retired CPA, a former radio talk show host, and was a professional orchestral musician. Currently she is an adjunct accounting professor.

Lisa is a graduate of Fuller Theological Seminary and holds two degrees from the University of Colorado. She is a vowed oblate in the Order of Julian of Norwich.

Calvin and Lisa have four children and are happy empty-nesters. They reside in Colorado.

For more information about Lisa Aré Wulf, please visit www.LisaAreWulf.com